MAD AT
GOD

FROM
SIGHING
TO
SINGING

The prophet Habakkuk portrays
recovery from Post-Traumatic Spiritual Disorder

Lee Milliner

ISBN 978-1-0980-8421-9 (paperback)
ISBN 978-1-0980-8422-6 (digital)

Christian Faith Publishing, Inc.
832 Park Avenue
Meadville, PA 16335
www.christianfaithpublishing.com

Printed in the United States of America

I dedicate this book to all the young men and women who considered the cost and answered the call to serve their country through military service. Many have paid the ultimate sacrifice and even more bear in their body, mind, and soul the consequences of combat.

FOREWORD

By Margaret Grun Kibben
Chaplain, House of Representatives
Rear Admiral, Chaplain Corps, USN (retired)
Twenty-sixth Chief of Navy Chaplains

The road to spiritual recovery is well-trod, but nonetheless lonely, long, and challenging. Faithful people have felt themselves shaken to the very foundation of belief upon which they once stood firmly and confidently, bereft of the certainty and security they once enjoyed. The questions that arise out of these spiritual crises are painful and overwhelming. And to whom does one pose them? To God? The very One who seems to have cursed them, or worse, abandoned them? Does one dare to serve as the Almighty's interlocutor? Won't that return some sort of divine judgment even worse than the predicament one now endures?

And so, one is left alone, hopeless, disheartened, and angry. Isolated from the love God promised. Hopeless that God would even deign to intervene. Disheartened that everything one believed about God and faith was an illusion. Angry that everything that seemed so safe and secure in God's everlasting arms has been thrown into chaos.

But this is the true tale of the journey of faith. And an ordinary guy, like Habakkuk, on his own life's path comes alongside each and every one of us on ours to share our pain to give voice to our distress. And through Habakkuk's own courageous confrontation with God, he shows us the way through.

For Habakkuk's story is ours as well. *Mad at God* unwraps the mystery of the Old Testament prophet's wisdom through Lee Milliner's own experience as a seasoned military chaplain and combat veteran, and we are given an invitation to peer into the soul of the despairing believer that we may find our own way through perplexity and pain. Heartfelt and heartrending, this book taps into the hard-earned wisdom of scripture in a way that is understandable and affirming. We are allowed to wrestle with the angst and anger that come with facing inexpressible pain and untold sorrow. There are no holds barred.

The current day images provided in this space are both real and eternal bringing the Old Testament world from which Habakkuk speaks into our own. His suffering, perplexity, and argument are the very cries we ourselves have made time and again. But what makes his such a powerful testimony is that even so, Habakkuk believes. It's clearly not an easy belief; Habakkuk taps into the depth of his soul and unearths his deepest pain and challenges God to prove His faithfulness.

Only then, after Habakkuk has laid himself bare before his Creator, does he take the next step into solitude and silence. It's here where he—and we—are called to listen, look, and wait for the Lord to speak. And with him we continue the journey into spiritual reflection and renewal.

In the face of all this, how then shall we live? How do we move forward? Habakkuk emerges from the depths with a tentative certainty (is this not what faith is after all?) that *shalom*, peace, wholeness, shall be restored if we are willing to risk yielding our will, our control, and our sense of how things *should* be to the gracious care of our Sovereign God. Habakkuk's story, the witness of Paul and the early Church, and the personal narrative shared within these chapters bring us—carefully, thoughtfully—to this place of surrender. And here is revealed the hope of healing and restoration.

This book tackles the one place few are willing to go: into the eye of the storm that is the crisis of faith. But it's here that recovery is received: real and available for all who have the courage to move toward the salvation found in our Redeemer.

ACKNOWLEDGMENTS

Special thanks to my navy chaplain colleague, friend, and old running partner Daniel Stewart for reviewing the manuscript and offering helpful suggestions. I want to thank my cycling partner and twenty-sixth chief of navy chaplains, Margaret Kibben, for reading the manuscript and writing the Foreword. Also, special thanks to Martin Negron who traveled with me throughout western Iraq as my trusted assistant and bodyguard and to my friend and deputy while in Fallujah, Alan Hansen, for his selfless devotion to duty as a combat chaplain. Finally, I want to acknowledge my wife for her tireless editing of the manuscript, for her sage advice concerning the content, and for her assistance in bringing this book to fruition. I also deeply appreciate the use of her original poetry.

INTRODUCTION

In 2007, I was diagnosed with post-traumatic stress disorder. I kept regular appointments with a navy psychiatrist and found some relief in the assortment of medications prescribed for me. Fortunately, my work as a navy chaplain was not impaired so I continued on active duty serving the young men and women who wear our nation's cloth with courage, pride, and honor.

I deployed to Anbar Province of Western Iraq to the city of Fallujah with Second Marine Expeditionary Force Forward for an eleven-month combat tour in 2005–2006. I was the force chaplain responsible for over ninety-five chaplains in Western Iraq. It was the best and the worst year of my life. The opportunity to provide religious ministry and pastoral care to young warriors who risked their lives every day was an honor like no other. I rode in hundreds of Marine and Army helicopters to visit the many camps and combat posts throughout our area of operations. Everywhere I visited, I spoke with military men and women who missed home but were committed to their jobs. Serving them as a navy chaplain was the highlight of my twenty-seven years of naval service—counseling, consoling, supporting, teaching, baptizing, and encouraging, constitute spiritual ministry of the highest order. Every day offered more opportunities to serve, and I cherished each occasion I was privileged to provide religious ministry and spiritual care. Most combat chaplains will agree that combat ministry is the apex of chaplaincy.

The year in Iraq was equally the most challenging year of my life. Listening day after day to the concerns of the warriors will take a toll on any counselor. Comforting wounded warriors and saying goodbye to warriors killed in action exacts an excruciating toll. Facing danger every time you travel outside the compound and hearing the constant sound of the artillery intensifies the toll. Riding in convoys as a back-seat passenger without a weapon can extract a fearsome toll. Also, incoming rounds make one more vigilant than normal. I left Iraq with the sights, smells, and sounds imbedded in my memory; these memories would soon become a distraction, later a disturbance and ultimately a disorder (PTSD). Robert Grant, in his book *The way of the wound: A spirituality of trauma and transformation*, speaks to "compassion fatigue" and "secondary traumatization."

> Those who constantly bear witness to the wounds of others absorb trauma vicariously.... Continually seeing or hearing stories of pain and horror can challenge a professional's basic belief about self and society, as well as his/her need to be competent and in control. (p. 14)

Anyone can experience post-traumatic stress disorder. It impacts males and females at all age levels. It is diagnosed in hundreds of thousands of people around the world. Dr. Charles Hoge points out in his book *Once a Warrior—Always a Warrior: Navigating the Transition from Combat to Home* that the

> development of PTSD after combat experiences has very little (or nothing) to do with the character, upbringing or genetics of the warrior." He states that "certain events are profoundly devastating and have a much stronger impact neurologically than others, a situation that the warrior has absolutely no control over. PTSD in these situations represents normal reactions to extremely abnormal (or extraordinary) events. (p. 38)

PTSD is broadly defined as a mental health condition that is triggered by exposure to an extremely terrifying event—either experiencing it or witnessing it or learning about it from friends or family. Symptoms may include flashbacks, nightmares, and severe anxiety, sleep disturbances, uncontrollable thoughts about the event, panic attacks, and other behaviors. In her book, *Pastoral Care for Post-Traumatic Stress Disorder*, Dalene Rogers quotes from the *Diagnostic and Statistical Manual of Mental Disorders* (2000) to describe the precipitating PTSD event.

> [E]xposure to an extreme traumatic stressor involving direct personal experience of an event that involves actual or threatened death or serious injury, or other threat to one's physical integrity; or witnessing an event that involves death, injury, or a threat to the physical integrity of another person; or learning about unexpected or violent death, serious hard, or threat of death or injury experience by a family member or other close associate (Criterion A1 (p. 463). Reprinted with permission from the Diagnostic and Statistical Manual of Mental Disorders Fourth Edition, Text Revision. Copyright 2000 American Psychiatric Association. (p. 2, 3)

From all external appearances, my combat tour was very successful. I was awarded the Legion of Merit for my leadership in combat ministry:

> For exceptionally meritorious conduct in the performance of outstanding service while serving as Force Chaplain, II Marine expeditionary Force (Forward), U. S. Marine Corps Forces, Central, from March 2005-January 2006 in support of Operation IRAQI FREEDOM 04-06. In this position of considerable responsibility, Captain Milliner crafted and implemented the religious

ministry support program for over 38,000 Marines, Sailors, Soldiers, and Airmen across the expanse of 26 camps and forward operating bases throughout western Iraq. His unparalleled knowledge of military ministry and United States Marine Corps culture made him a model of mentorship for the 95 Religious Ministry Teams and a trusted colleague to the entire Marine expeditionary Force (Forward) staff.... From the development of the II Marine expeditionary force (Forward) religious ministry plan to the supervision and mentorship of 95 chaplain and 97 religious support personnel providing religious support in combat operation. Captain Milliner has met every challenge with skill, insight, innovation, and teamwork. Captain Milliner's dynamic direction, keen judgment, and inspiring devotion to duty reflected great credit upon him and upheld the highest tradition of the United States Naval Service.

For the President
M. W. Hagee
Commandant of the Marine Corps

By all accounts, it looked like I was at the peak of my profession, but much was happening below the external markings of success. The mental anguish, post-traumatic stress, and spiritual unrest were just beginning to surface and impact the quality of my life.

I decided to retire from the navy in 2008. A coveted position had opened up at Campbell University, and I knew that this would probably be my only opportunity to apply for it. I also thought that leaving the military environment might abate some of my symptoms. I was selected and hired for the position of Director in the Campbell University's Extended Campus at Marine Corps Base Camp Lejeune and Marine Corps Air Station New River. I also taught *Introduction to Christianity* and *Christian Ethics* for Campbell University as adjunct faculty and *Old Testament Survey* at Coastal Carolina Community College. Additionally, I served as interim pastor for First Baptist Church in Maysville, North Carolina, and for Bear Creek Baptist Church in Hubert, North Carolina. The change was welcomed, and I immensely enjoyed teaching young men and women and leading a faculty and staff to provide the best higher educational opportunity in our local area. But my office was on a military base and the frequent sound of distant mortar rounds and helicopter flyovers took me back to Iraq often and unexpectedly. I served in this capacity for five years. My PTSD symptoms did not lessen.

The symptoms I experienced are typical for anyone suffering with post-traumatic stress disorder. Like many others, I found it very difficult to seek mental health care. Though the military has done a remarkable job of removing any stigma attached to seeking mental health assistance, it is still very difficult to admit to another human being that your personal coping skills are not adequate for what you are facing today. Who wants to admit to failure? After months of sleep problems, nightmares, panic attacks, and hypervigilance, I knew I needed some help, but it was a frightening flashback that sent me to sick call to ask for a mental health assessment. I am glad I went. I do not hesitate to recommend mental health services to others. The prescribed medicine and the psychiatrist's insights provided me some stability, but not healing. And the persistent "why" questions I entertained led to an even deeper challenge: spiritual trauma.

I began this book over nine years ago. I had to table it because of the emotional and mental anguish the memories stirred. Recently, I decided to visit the material and begin to write again. It has been a painful process as long-buried memories, conversations, sights, sounds, and experiences have appeared in my dreams, nightmares, and thoughts. Although causing anguish I had not experienced in a while, the writing has been therapeutic.

Daily, I read the stories of families sharing their pain due to the ravaging effects of COVID-19 across the American landscape.

The "why" questions multiply by the hour. Pastors, church members, and devoted disciples of Christ suffer like everyone else. They are not exempt from germs or virus or human disease. Yet oftentimes their spiritual questions are more painful and persistent than the problems. Those who believe in God and the Bible will encounter questions differently from those with purely secular beliefs. These are questions that challenge faith and devotion. This is spiritual trauma.

Spiritual Trauma

I was on my first tour of duty in San Diego, California, when I received word that my good friend and seminary colleague was tragically killed an overseas plane crash. He had preached my ordination sermon and we had forged a close relationship during our seminary days. We both pastored small rural churches within an hour of each other. Upon graduation, he received a call to missions in Uruguay. He and his young family moved to Costa Rica for a year of intensive Spanish language study. Then they committed to full-time missionary residence in country. He had prepared long and hard for this opportunity to teach the Bible and to start churches in a missionary setting. He had the personality, the training and skills, and the missionary gift. Then, one foggy day, in transit to a pastors' conference, his passenger plane collided with the side of a mountain. There were no survivors. In one sudden, unthinkably horrific accident, his life with its potential for good and for God was gone. He served only two years in the mission field before his death. Surely, he made a difference in those two years, but I grieved to consider how much more he could have accomplished for the Lord.

After recovering from the shock, I wrestled a long time with my personal perplexity and pain. "Why?" I asked over and over again. "How could God allow this to happen to one who was so committed to doing good for others and to making a positive difference in the world?" The patented answers that the church and Christians normally give on such occasions such as "it must have been God's will" just didn't satisfy my soul's anguish. In fact, I really came to resist and rebuke such quick answers to the painful questions of the soul.

It was during this time that I discovered *Habakkuk*; this prophet and prophetic word has since been my soul's solace. In this book, I found bedrock truths that can sustain any soul in the darkest days of distress and despair. I learned how to embrace my questions, not to detest them. I learned how to pray about my questions, not to deny them. I learned how one can have questions with no answers and at the same time have faith in a good and all-powerful God. I learned how to move beyond the questions of my soul to the eternal truth of Scripture and to an encounter of the truly awesome God. Only then could I understand, and in unison with Habakkuk, sing his psalm of praise in chapter 3. But the journey is not over. There are many days and times when I must return to this Old Testament prophet to renew my faith once again, for life is filled with circumstances and crises that present even more questions than answers.

My battles with a barrage of questions with no answers led me on a personal quest to discover some truth that could sustain me and others during these painful periods of perplexity. I was frequently contemplating, "What do we do when our questions find no answers? What do we do when we are puzzled by the problems we encounter, perplexed by the pain we must bear and overpowered by the pressure we feel? What do we do when answers are sought, but none are found?" My struggles led me to Habakkuk where I discovered a word from God for all the questions and seasons of life.

For twenty-seven years, I served as a chaplain in the United States Navy. Whether on a ship at sea, a submarine in port, or with sailors and their families at military bases in the United States or overseas, I have been asked and pleaded with to answer these questions that have no answers. Delivering the messages to inform sailors of a family member's accident or death always means such questions will be vocalized. I have been hit, shaken, screamed at, and cried upon as people express their pain and ask those questions for which I have no answers. Serving with the Marines for seventeen of my twenty-seven years, I have heard these soul-wrenching questions from young Marines in tents, on field marches, in the office, at the hospital and wherever Marines, their spouses and their children live and work. The uniqueness of navy chaplaincy is our mission to be with the Marines and Sailors in their workspaces at sea or on shore and to be easily accessible to them twenty-four hours a day. Therefore, the questions come very often, during the day and night, and with the questions come an expectation that the chaplain will have an answer. Even those who have no religious preference seek out the chaplain in times of distress to ask the questions that are tormenting the mind. I have often thought that military chaplains are always stationed on the "front lines" of spiritual conflict. Though the military member and their families don't often recognize it, the questions asked daily of chaplains are spiritual. "How can I function, work, and go on living with these painful questions?" They desire answers—even demand answers from the chaplain who is viewed as the institutional representative of religious faith and of God. They expect that he or she will be able to speak to their concerns, quell the anguish of their soul, and with some God-inspired word of wisdom, make life bearable, manageable and worthwhile for them. And I have found it most difficult to resist the easy answers such as "God has a purpose," "Must be God's will," or "It is for the best" and instead embrace and respect their questions and humbly admit—openly and honestly—that I have no answers. But I confess that my willingness to be honest has opened up the doors for more authentic ministry and the sharing of faith that I discovered in Habakkuk.

I am now persuaded that the spiritual trauma caused by the barrage of questions that have no satisfying answers is a serious issue for many people of faith: *Why doesn't God heal? Why doesn't God intervene and change these circumstances? What good is prayer if God doesn't answer? I am a faithful, devoted Christian, yet look what I have to endure whereas I know unbelievers who have it made.* The questions are endless; they are heart wrenching and soul disturbing. I provide no answers to the questions. Neither does Habakkuk. But Habakkuk does show us how to move from being mad at God and sighing to a faith in God with singing in and through the questions and pain of life.

I am convinced that spiritual trauma can be as severe as psychological trauma. It was for me. Judith Herman in *Trauma and Recovery* makes this observation: "All forms of trauma—sexual, physical, and psychological—have an effect on one's spirituality. Some people have said that spiritual trauma has had the most lasting and devastating impact on their lives" (p. 8). She further describes what spiritual trauma does to a person:

> Spiritual trauma attacks the core of one's being; one relationship to God and the relationship to oneself. The meaning and purpose of life becomes vague, confused, or lost. The ability to connect with nature, mystery, love, people, the transcendent, is ruptured, and the effects of such brokenness surface. (p. 8)

Upon my return from Fallujah, Iraq, I continued to visit our wounded Marines and soldiers at Landstuhl Regional Medical Center in Kaiserslautern, Germany; Brooke Army Medical Center at Fort Sam Houston, Texas; and Walter Reed National Medical Center, in Washington, DC. I heard over and over again their stories of combat and their painful journey. I heard their anguish of soul. These young people had served voluntarily and now they faced uncertain futures with physical, mental, emotional, and spiritual challenges most cannot imagine. Their suffering and struggles only added to my own questions about God and faith and intensified my spiritual trauma.

Trauma can be any event of such deep intensity that it actually breaks down our personal defenses and overwhelms us with acute anxiety, confusion, and bewilderment. Often, the traumatic event is re-experienced in our dreams or nightmares. There are recurrent and intrusive recollections of the event. The emotions attached to the event can resurface at any time—sometimes in unexpected ways, places and in similar events. The disturbance can cause significant distress and impairment of our normal means of coping and functioning. Hoge observes, "Numerous things can trigger reactions of anxiety, fear, and anger, or result in the warrior suddenly being flooded with images and feelings, bringing the war zone home or the warrior back to the war zone" (p. 135). Trauma can be significantly severe if it continues beyond several months.

Judith Herman in her book *Trauma and Recovery* states that "[t]raumatic events call into question basic human relationships.... They undermine the belief systems that give meaning to human experience. They violate the victim's faith in a natural or divine order and cast the victim into a state of existential crisis" (p. 51).

I suffered from combat trauma. I would have expected my Christian faith in a good and gracious God to lead to a quick recovery. However, when my faith in God was questioned, it only compounded the complete array of symptoms. My spiritual life and faith in God was the bedrock of my soul and when it was disturbed, I was in deeper distress.

Post-traumatic spiritual disorder occurs when we continue to question God, our faith and our entire belief system that has sustained us throughout life's experiences. When we no longer find meaning in our worship and in our spiritual rituals, and we harbor unresolved anger toward God, ours becomes a spiritual disorder. There may be a loss of hope and trust. Feelings of guilt and shame may overpower us when we believe we are betraying our religious faith. Our negativity toward God and religion affects those closest to us. This may create an unwanted emotional distance. Those who know us in the faith community may be concerned, but if we don't return quickly to our place of worship, we may be left alone by those we need the most. Loneliness may set in as we distance ourselves from others and from God. Losing one's faith in all that has been taught and practiced as a Christian is possible. I know those who have never recovered from it. Their anger toward God has led them to disown their religious faith and to discard all remnants of their past spiritual life. Dalene Rogers observes, "They may disavow the goodness of humanity.... Spiritual losses also may be reflected in a lack of hope in the future, the loss of trust, a sense of no longer being a whole person, the inability to respond spontaneously and optimistically,…" (p. 19). If people do not recover from spiritual trauma, then life begins to reflect the dissolution of their faith. Spiritual renewal and recovery from spiritual trauma is as important as any recovery from the psychological impacts of the trauma upon our well-being. In fact, I believe that recovery from post-traumatic spiritual disorder is essential to meaning and purpose in life and critical to dealing with post-traumatic stress. Habakkuk shows us how to move from sighing to singing. The prophet starts out mad at God, expressing without regret, but he ends his book with a marvelous song of praise to God.

I have written this book for those who ask questions of God and of their religious leaders and receive no satisfying answers. Like me, their quest for answers has often led to discouragement, to doubt and to depression. The heavens sometimes appear to be silent to the soul's screaming, and they don't know where they can legitimately turn with their questions. I hope you will discover the same spiritual strength from Habakkuk's prophetic word as I. Raymond Calkins, in his book *The Modern Message of the Minor Prophets* states, "There is no Old Testament book that is able to do more for the burdened souls of men or to raise them to higher levels of hope and confidence than the brief prophecy of Habakkuk" (p. 92).

Recovery from spiritual trauma is as important as recovery from the psychological impacts of the trauma upon our well-being.

CHAPTER 1

The Perplexity of the Prophet

Questions and Answers

Finding the Old Testament prophetic book of *Habakkuk* may require the use of the Bible's index. Tucked among the twelve "minor prophets," *Habakkuk* has often been overlooked as readers and students desire to get to the larger and more well-known "major" prophets. The size of the prophetic writing and the status of the prophet, however, do not determine the importance of the prophet's message. Consisting of only three chapters, *Habakkuk's* value is far greater than its small size.

The seventh-century BC prophet Habakkuk lived and ministered during a time of turmoil in the small nation of Judah. Israel to the north had been subjected to the military advances of Tiglathpileser III and his great Assyrian army. Israel and its capital Samaria fell to the Assyrians in 721 BC, and the people of Israel were scattered within the Assyrian empire. Judah had survived the Assyrian conquests but was required to pay a heavy tax to Assyria which took an economic toll on the kingdom and its people.

The Chaldeans mentioned in 1:6 challenged the Assyrians, and ultimately its great capital Nineveh fell in 612 BC. Judah soon became a vassal state of these conquerors but survived until 587 BC when Judah and its capital Jerusalem fell to the invading armies of the Babylonians (Chaldeans). Though opinions vary and the book provides only a few hints as to date, it can be argued that the prophet Habakkuk ministered in the period after the fall of Nineveh, the capital of Assyria (612 BC) and before the destruction of Jerusalem and the fall of the kingdom of Judah (587 BC). Baily and Barker in their *The New American Commentary: Micah, Nahum, Habakkuk, Zephaniah* conclude, "It was an agitated time, characterized by rapid political change, international turmoil, bloody military encounters, and a growing rebellion against the demands of the covenant by the great majority in Judah" (p. 251).

The prophet witnessed the moral and spiritual degeneracy in Judah and the demise of law and order. He saw the increase in violence, the weakening of judicial authority and the inattention to the moral and legal code of their religion. Habakkuk intuitively knew that Judah was a dying nation and he could not understand why God didn't intervene to change the course of destruction.

Chapter 1 of Habakkuk clearly communicates the perplexity of the prophet in the content of the prophet's prayer. The prophet presents his protest to God in sincere and reverent prayer. He could not understand why the circumstances in Judah were being allowed to deteriorate. Each day he witnessed the turmoil in his country; the burden for his beloved land and its people grew greater. He prayed passionately to God.

God Hears Our Prayers

Before consideration is given to the content of the prophet's prayer, we need to understand a basic premise behind the prayer of this prophet. It is so basic that it is often sadly ignored or simply assumed. The prophet believed that God hears prayers and that God heard his prayerful petitions. Here is the altar on which every prayer must be offered. The style of prayer, the position of prayer, the language of prayer, even the substance of prayer—none of these things seriously mattered to this prophet in pain. Of paramount importance is a simple (even childlike) belief that God hears his prayers.

Though Habakkuk could not understand why things were happening the way they were and why God would allow these things to occur, he never wavered in his bold belief that his God heard him whenever he prayed. If not, why pray? If one didn't believe that God heard prayers, then prayer would in fact be an exercise in futility. Therefore, though an elementary element, this belief is foundational to our faith and pivotal for the practice of prayer.

God hears us when we pray. It doesn't matter if we are in church, by our beds at night, or in our cars driving to and from work. It doesn't matter if we whisper our prayers, shout out our prayers, or pray silently in our mind and heart—God hears our prayers. Even though there are millions of us praying at the same time and from all continents of the world, God hears our individual prayers. I can't explain it or fathom it, but I believe it. So did the prophet Habakkuk. That is why he prayed. That is why we pray. It is what gives importance to the act of prayer, and it is the impetus for prayer. The belief that we can speak to the Supreme Being from our soul, believing that our words are heard and that their meaning will never be lost in translation, is fundamental to understanding prayer. To Habakkuk and all who pray, this is the mystery and miracle of prayer. God hears the words and God hears all that is behind those words. The prophet Jeremiah proclaimed, "For surely I know the plans I have for you, says the Lord, plans for your welfare and not for harm, to give a future with hope. Then when you call upon me and pray to me, I will hear you. When you search for me, you will find me; if you seek me with all of your heart" (29:11–13).

There are those times when we have to repeat this profound belief to ourselves to reinforce its meaning, "God hears my prayers! Yes, God hears my prayers." Feelings may indicate otherwise. We may sense that God is absent from us and the eerie silence is too much for us to endure. We look for indications in every direction that our prayer is being heard, but there are no assurances. We seriously speculate that perhaps our prayers are a waste, so why pray? These are indeed painful times when we must state emphatically, "God hears my prayers." The power of these words cited over and over again can clear our soul of doubt's fog and unleash our spirit to sense God's presence.

I have counseled with numerous people who questioned whether God was hearing their prayers. They needed reassurance from a minister. Their emotions of anger, disappointment, grief, and depression were blocking any feelings of goodness, love, kindness, and grace. Therefore, they incorrectly assumed that God was far removed from their pain, oblivious to their predicament, and deaf to their petitions. Their emotional pain simply interfered with their sensing the presence of God. Unable to sense intuitively God's presence, they thought that God had rejected them and refused to hear their prayers. The darkness of God's apparent neglect and His silence blackened their skies and they saw negative everywhere. The reassurance they sought from a minister was that God was indeed hearing their prayers in spite of missing evidence. The chaplain can communicate care and compassion. Rodgers observes, "God calls us to walk with the wounded as living reminders of God's love; offering guidance, support, and hope for the spiritual journey to full recovery. This is soul work—heart work—and demands the best of us" (p. 106).

I have asked people to do a simple recitation for several minutes before they pray, "God hears my prayers." I have suggested that they visualize God sitting on a celestial throne listening to them. Most have reported back to me that it made a tremendous difference in their prayers. Reciting "God hears my prayers" and visualizing God leaning over and listening to them made it much easier to perceive that God was hearing them and being attentive to their concerns.

I was asked to supervise a new chaplain on his first tour of duty. He had deployed with his unit for six months. Several months into the deployment, it became apparent to the senior chaplain that his wife was becoming involved with another man. Thus, he was brought home immediately and informed of his wife's behavior. All concerned hoped that they could work through their issues.

Upon his arrival home, he was shocked to discover that his wife had allowed a Marine to move into their house. She did not deny what she had done and stated that the affair would continue. He was devastated. He had been engaged in Christian ministry to the men and women of the Marine Corps, sacrificing for God and country, and this happened. The senior chaplain assigned him to me and asked that I serve as his supervisory chaplain and provide pastoral care to him.

He wanted desperately to save his marriage and family, but his wife refused all attempts to salvage their relationship. She asked for a divorce and left Hawaii with the Marine who had been disciplined and discharged for his adulterous affair. He was alone in an empty apartment with a lot of memories and his grief to bear.

The next year would be one of the most difficult in my years of Christian ministry as I sought to provide spiritual ministry to the troops in my units and to him. Never before had I witnessed such intense and prolonged grief and loneliness. His questions of God were profound and painstakingly honest. Yes, he wanted to know why God would let this happen and how God could let it happen. This minister knew the Scriptures and the answers normally given in such circumstances. But finding himself in the pit of perplexity and the abyss of anguish, he could not find any solace in Scripture or serenity in prayer.

His recovery required time and counseling. I had to stop him from doing any couples' counseling because those he counseled complained of his negativity toward marriage. Healing for him began when he could personally affirm once again that God was not absent, but listening to his prayers. He would practice repeating phrases which stated that God was hearing his prayers. He would visualize God listening to his prayers. Then, the day came when he actually could trust and testify that God was indeed hearing his prayers. This was an emotional breakthrough and a spiritual deliverance. He could once again pray, trusting that God was listening; he was able to face his perplexity and pain, share it with God, and begin to feel the Holy Spirit working to heal his hurts.

I was blessed to watch God heal a broken heart and restore a man of God to the ministry of caring for hurting persons. He later remarried to a beautiful and kind Christian lady and resumed his ministry as a chaplain. I learned during this difficult year what I had taken for granted for many years, that really believing God hears our prayers is often the portal to the presence of God. In her book *Pastoral Care for Post-Traumatic Stress Disorder: Healing the Shattered Soul*, Rogers observes, "Contemplative prayer is a time of quietness with the anticipation of discovery of one's relationship with God as a beloved child. The potential to heal shame and other spiritual wounds is infinite. By resting in God's presence and affirming God's love, burdens may be unloaded" (p. 40). Peter in his first epistle instructs Christians to cast all their anxiety upon Christ because He cares for them (1 Peter 5:7).

There is an old Christian classic that I remember singing as a youth, "Leave it There":

> *Leave it there, leave it there*
> *Just take your burden to the Lord oh and leave it*
> *   there*
> *If you trust him through your doubt, He will surely*
> *   bring you out*
> *Take your burden to the Lord, leave it there*
> *Now if your body suffers pain and your health you*
> *   can't regain*
> *And your soul is slowly sinking in despair*
> *Jesus knows the pain you feel, He can save and He*
> *   can heal*
> *Take your burden to the Lord, leave it there.*

Paul, in his *Letter to the Philippians*, exhorts "be not be anxious about anything, but in everything, by prayer and petition, with thanksgiving, present your requests to God" (Philippians 4:6). It is evident, then, that to these New Testament writers, taking one's burdens, anxieties, requests, and petitions to God is vitally important. In fact, Paul goes on the say that "the peace of God, which transcends all understanding, will guard your hearts and your minds in Christ

Jesus." Paul states that the peace of God will set watch upon your heart and mind as a result of prayer.

God Listens to Our Complaints

Even a cursory reading of Habakkuk chapter 1 reveals the prophet's faith that his prayer to God is heard. But it also shows us another component of Habakkuk's belief about prayer. Habakkuk believed that God permitted an honest expression of his feelings and his pain. I really like this. It took a long while in my life for me to understand and appreciate this truth. From Habakkuk, we learn that it is all right to say to God whatever is on our mind. Habakkuk was confused that God was allowing violence, evil, and trouble to continue in the land. Habakkuk told God exactly how he felt. He directed the questions of his soul directly to God: "Why?" "How long shall I cry?" He held nothing back. Jewish theologian Abraham Heschel noted, "We are closer to God when we are asking questions than when we think we have the answers." And I think to Habakkuk's own surprise and amazement, God never rebuked him or condemned him for his questions or complaint. Nowhere in the Bible do we find that God rejects a person's prayer when prayed in the language of lament. Habakkuk was stating to God what was tormenting his mind and crushing his soul. He gave words to his perplexity and pain. He addressed those words to his God. His God heard him and responded without any retribution.

I don't know about you, but this really means something to me. When I stand with people in pain who cry out to God and proceed to apologize to me for doing so, I can with confidence state that it is all right. God permits us to be honest and open with our feelings. God permits us to ask "why." God permits us to scream and cry and express our anger and sadness. God permits us to be human. Mary Margaret Funk noted in *Thoughts Matter: Discover the Spiritual Journey*, "When tears come, I breathe deeply and rest. I know I am swimming in a hallowed stream where many have gone before. I am not alone, crazy, or having a nervous breakdown…. My heart is at work. My soul is awake" (p. 137).

I find it interesting that in the first verse of chapter 2, Habakkuk says that he will retire to his place of solitude and "watch to see what He will say to me, and what I will answer when I am corrected." The prophet expected a word of condemnation from God. Questioning God is not something the prophets usually did. But no such condemnation came to Habakkuk. Why? Because God truly understands the human condition and He permits a free expression of our feelings and concerns to Him in sincere and honest prayer. I am glad that there are no subjects and no feelings out of bounds in prayer. God permits and expects us to pray what is on our hearts and minds.

God Answers Our Prayers

Habakkuk believed that God would answer him. It is not enough for us to believe that God permits us to say what is on our mind. It is not enough for us to believe that God hears us when we pray to him. Instead, we must follow Habakkuk to a much higher truth that God will answer prayer. If we don't go this far in our belief, then prayer can be limited to a kind of emotional, mental, and spiritual therapy. Yes, it may make us feel better, even cope better, but we miss the something more. We miss God's word for us and God's blessing for us.

Now, we all know that even though we believe God answers prayer, the answer may not be what we want, what we think we need, or what we expect. Far too often, our view of prayer is like the boy the preacher overheard saying, "Tokyo, Tokyo, Tokyo." The minister asked why he was saying "Tokyo" over and over again. The boy responded that he just had to make an A on his geography test and he was praying that God would make Tokyo the capital of France. I am afraid that this young boy missed that question and misunderstood the complexities of prayer.

The truth is that sometimes God does change circumstances for us. The truth is that sometimes God protects us from danger with or without our knowledge. Yes, sometimes God chooses to heal emotional, mental, and physical illness and pain. Sometimes, however, He does not. But He always answers our prayers. We need to learn to look for those answers; to look for that word from God; to look for that blessing from God. Who knows how the answer may come, what form the answer may take, what person may be the instrument of God's answer? In chapter 1 of Habakkuk, God told the prophet that he is using the "terrible and dreadful" Chaldeans as his answer. God can use anything and anyone to send an answer our way. The answer may not be what we are looking expectantly for, but we can be assured that our prayers are answered. In fact, we may never see the answer to our prayer, but this doesn't mean the prayers have not been answered.

A young sailor's wife came to see me about a recent miscarriage. She had recovered physically, but not emotionally and spiritually. Her physician had recommended that she schedule an appointment with the chaplain. She clearly presented a spiritual problem. Her guilt was overwhelming. The cause of the guilt was her persistent question of "why." Her religious upbringing had taught her that it was wrong to question the tragedies of life. She stated that she could not help it. She believed that there was probably a reason for what had happened, but she could not help wondering and asking, "Why?" However, the more she asked "why," the greater her guilt. Her guilt was causing her to isolate herself from others, withdraw from her husband and silently bear her personal pain. I introduced her to Habakkuk. She was shocked to learn that a man of God could talk to God like that. We talked more about prayer and Habakkuk's authentic expression of his soul's pain to God. She promised to give it a try.

Several weeks later, we met for a follow-up, and she was pleasantly surprised at how well she was feeling. Even though it was extremely difficult for her, she finally opened up her soul and honestly spilled out all her feelings about what had transpired in her life. The more she said to God, the easier it became, and before long, she stated that she was sharing concerns and questions to God that she had kept tucked away inside for many years. The sense of relief was evident on her face. She had learned a very valuable component to prayer. To her, if for no other reason, her personal tragedy had brought her to a place of peace about many past pains. Habakkuk had given to this young lady a different view of prayer that freed her from guilt and favored her with the blessing of God.

I have counseled many people who have held on to anger toward God for years. To them, God had let them down. He had betrayed them. Some tragic event in their life for which they could find no reason led them to direct all their negative feelings toward God. They were mad at God, and they could not find resolution. Unresolved, the anger was directed toward the church, ministers, and Christians. Some of the most outspoken critics of Christians and the church have been those who have unresolved anger toward God. Hurting people are inclined to hurt people. They pass on their anger to others. As time passes without intervention, it becomes extremely difficult for them to recognize the source of their anger and to get help for it.

This is one reason I believe it is very important for people to talk about their anger toward God and for ministers and other care givers to create the opportunity for them to express their perplexity and pain. Most Christians find it very uncomfortable communicating to a minister or counselor their anger toward God. People have apologized time and time to me after an outburst of anger toward God as though such actions are inappropriate for Christians. They usually find comfort in my remarks that God takes no offense to their painful protests of divine providence. Healing of these damaged emotions occurs as they honestly reflect on these feelings and own them as legitimate.

The Prophet's Prayer

Little is known about the man Habakkuk. Several clues in the book, however, help us to form a picture of the prophet. Though not detailed, the image is sufficient to aid in the understanding of his writing.

Habakkuk was a prophet. In the first verse of the book, the Hebrew term *nabi* is utilized to describe him. Though a common term for *prophet*, it is sparingly used in this manner. Indications from biblical research are that the term employed here in the title is a technical term ("the prophet") to denote a specific role or ministry. It is widely believed that Habakkuk was a prophet who performed his ministry at the Jerusalem temple, providing oracles and songs for worship. Throughout the book, musical and liturgical directions are given indicating that the material is to be used in worship.

Habakkuk was burdened for his nation and its people. He spoke from his own pain, but he also represented the righteous in his nation. Their concerns were his concerns and as a representative of the people, he shares their questions with God. So unusual is his technique that he has been called "the father of speculation in Israel. With him religion goes prominently into the interrogation mood" (Patterson, p. 131). Some have even suggested that he is more philosopher than prophet. While the language and style of the book is similar to the writings of the sages and singers of Israel, Habakkuk is a prophet who interrogates God, hoping for an answer to proclaim to the community of faith. Habakkuk's impassioned pleas and protests to God are to understand so he can make known God's will to the faithful. He is aware of the concerns of those who are faithful to the covenant faith; he wants to give them answers from God. His is the heart of a prophet, passionate to proclaim the purpose of God. Though communicated in the language of the Psalms, his proclamation of faith in chapter 3 is a word of comfort and hope for the people in a desperate time.

I believe that the prayers of Habakkuk identify a special function of those prophets who ministered in teamwork with priests and psalmists at the temple and other religious sites. The prophets provided intercessory prayer on behalf of the people. To be sure, the primary role is the delivery of the "word of the Lord" to the people, but the role of intercessor is often overlooked. Habakkuk's prayer is personal and communal. He speaks to God on behalf of the people.

Their perplexity and pain are his; perhaps, the people even joined with him in offering these laments to God.

The book begins with a statement indicating that the prophet Habakkuk had a burden. Even though the Hebrew term is often employed to mean *oracle*, I think the literal translation of *burden* is appropriate. Verse 1: "The burden which Habakkuk the prophet did see." This man of God had a crushed heart. He carried a heavy burden because of what he saw in his own land and what he envisioned as the answer of God. His burden was the pain of perplexity. This burden has been shared by multitudes; most of whom silently bear it.

The pain of perplexity is the burden of many people. Daily (since we have twenty-four-hour news stations), we hear about terrible events and tragic circumstances that target our fundamental faith in a good and all-powerful God. Natural disasters strike with devastating destruction and recurring regularity (I personally have experienced Hurricanes Bertha, Fran, Bonnie, Floyd, and Dennis). Violence and crime exist without any sign of stopping. Global problems are multiplying. They challenge natural resources; divide people, religions and nations, and jeopardize international peace. Personally, we experience our own confusion, conflicts, and crises. Perplexity pervades our personal lives. And we wonder, "Where is God in all of this?" A spiritual struggle ensues among our beliefs about God, the world and our experience of life. Perplexed, we often deny our soul-gripping questions and choose to defend vigorously our long-held beliefs to avoid spiritual doubt and personal distress. Some brave the unknown waters of honest and courageous reflection and seriously wonder about their religious beliefs and even wrestle with those ideas, images, and impressions left by childhood training about God, the Bible, and the world. Often, those Christians who attempt to navigate the dangerous waters of perplexity about God and faith are criticized and condemned as being "weaker" Christians or rebellious sinners who do not accept at face value the Word of God. Therefore, honest and open questioning is discouraged and even denounced by many leaders and laity of the Christian faith. This belief is contrary to Scripture.

Listen to the Psalmist in Psalm 10, "Why do you stand afar off, O Lord? Why do you hide in times of trouble? The wicked in his pride persecutes the poor; Let them be caught in the plots which they have devised." And Psalm 13: "How long, O Lord? Will you forget me forever? How long will you hide your face from me? How long shall I take counsel in my soul, having sorrow in my heart daily? How long will my enemy be exalted over me?"

In the Book of Psalms, the so-called "Prayer Book of the Bible," there are more laments than any other prayer type. The laments were petitions directed to God prompted by some distress encountered by the person. The people of Israel did not hesitate to complain to God about their distress. They did so privately and publicly. These prayers were part of their worship service.

In my ministry as a church pastor and navy chaplain, I have listened to the cries of hundreds as they confront their personal questions of faith with no answers, and they cry, "Chaplain, Why?" Why is God doing this to me?" For many of these suffering people, God is viewed as the abuser in the relationship of faith: "God did this to me" or "God is responsible for this." I am asked or pleaded with to explain or defend God as hurting persons seek some meaning to their hurt. As the persons and stories multiply, so do the unanswered questions. I have turned with weakened faith and sometimes paralyzing doubt time and time again to the prophet Habakkuk for revelation and renewal of faith. You see, Habakkuk goes where few prophets have gone. He questions the prophetic word given to him by God. Without apology, he unabashedly presents his complaint directly to God.

I remember a humbling experience as a young student missionary visiting India for a summer. On one occasion, I was speaking to high school students attending an international school for missionary children. In my sincere attempt to convince these bright high school students of the validity of the Christian faith, I presented a very syrupy-sweet Gospel. I implied that following Christ would enhance the enrichment of life and eliminate the experience of suffering. Though my intentions were good and my motivations pure,

I overly dramatized what they could expect if they decided to commit to Christian discipleship. The resident missionary offered a firm admonition to me that evening. She clearly indicated that I was giving the impression that to be Christian meant saying farewell to a life of suffering and hardship. Her teaching, though embarrassing and painful at the time, was noted and instructive.

As human beings, Christians not excluded, we cannot sail the seas of life without confronting questions—perplexing, painful questions, sometimes overpowering questions, and often we find no answers to our searching. We desire answers and at times demand from God answers, but there may be only silence. It sometimes appears that God is a divine puppeteer and we are but puppets on a string. It sometimes appears we are but victims of fate, with no adequate answers, only questions and confusion. The "whys" and questions of life appear to be never ending. We cannot escape them; we cannot bury our heads in the sands of our religious faith and deny them. They confront us directly, often head on. No human being will escape this confrontation; someday, sometime, somewhere, we will each one confront circumstances we don't understand, questions we cannot answer, pain and suffering that appear to have no justification—no rhyme or reason; and we can join the multitudes who cry, "Why? Why, God?"

Most recently, I have read multiple accounts of Christian pastors who are struggling financially, emotionally, mentally, and spiritually because of the COVID crisis. With no church gatherings for an extended time, many churches have to cut staff and even reduce the pastor's salary. Pastors are caught between those who want the church doors opened immediately and those who insist that the doors remain closed. Many have been so adamant in their opinions that they have threatened to leave the church if their opinion is not selected. Pastors have members who are sick and dying with the virus. Many are tired, weak, and spiritually destitute.

In an opinion piece in *Baptist News Global*, August 18, 2020, Jakob Topper shared a Zoom call he conducted with ten pastors across three denominations. Four of the ten had confessed to recent suicidal ideations. Seeking to serve the people who often are the ones who turn against them can be spirit crushing. These veteran pastors share the emotional and spiritual toll the pandemic is having upon churches and church leaders. They are in the throes of post-traumatic spiritual stress with their "Why God?" questions multiplying. Topper stated, "Leading anxious congregations amidst a pandemic, a hyper-partisan culture, a civil rights movement, and an upcoming election is destroying the lives of our pastors. Literally."

Like these pastors, we have these questions and we don't know what to do with them. They frighten us. We are sometimes afraid to give voice to our faltering faith. Some think that to verbalize the questions may lead to some punishment—the proverbial strike of lightening—so we keep silent until we can hold it in no longer. These questions stagger our step and challenge our faith. But from Habakkuk we learn that it is all right to present our complaints to God in prayer. He did! We can!

During my time in Iraq, the insurgents began a much different approach to fighting the much superior Multi-National Force. They began to employ the IED (improvised explosive device). In the beginning, it was simply constructed and strategically placed in roadways where the weight of vehicles would set it off. Initially, they were more a nuisance than anything else because the explosive content was minimal. However, they began to develop more sophisticated IEDs with more powerful explosive material. These new and improved devices could be detonated by hand from a person at a safe distance from the road. Every road became hazardous. Every trip was fraught with anxiety and trepidation. A Marine driver told me that his job was the scariest and most dangerous in Iraq. I believed him.

Early on in my deployment, a Marine officer remarked to me during breakfast, "You know that you chaplains are high value targets of the enemy. Can you imagine what they could do to our morale if a chaplain was captured and tortured and placed on social media?" This did nothing to relieve my anxiety as my trusted assistant and protector, Master Chief Negron, and I traveled. It was a constant thought.

One hot day in Fallujah, I walked with the commanding general to a large field that contained the "graveyard" of damaged and destroyed military vehicles. I stood there and wondered about the occupants in those vehicles. Did they survive? What were their wounds? How are they today? So many vehicles and each one had carried two or more passengers. It was a sobering moment.

One of my chaplains was traveling in a Marine vehicle when it was hit by an IED. He was thrown from the vehicle, but injured. I met him several months ago and he is still dealing with the physical, psychological, and spiritual trauma of that tragic day. The chaplains did not hesitate to expose themselves to danger on a daily basis. Their fear did not deter them from going to outposts to visit their Marines and Soldiers and to provide opportunities for them to practice their religious faith. They would face their demons later.

The use of the IED by the enemy was an effective means to inflict damage to the Marines and Soldiers with little risk on their part. They had discovered a weakness and the means to exploit it. Our military vehicles were not equipped at the time for these explosions. The danger was on every road. At any time, a vehicle could be hit and another Marine or soldier maimed. It impacted the morale of the warriors. They would much rather face the enemy in direct combat than to face such unknowns while in a vehicle. Many confessed their fear of driving or riding on the roads. "Could this be my day? I have been fortunate so far, but today may be different." Many would come to the chaplains for small New Testaments or religious emblems to carry with them. Convoys wanted the chaplain to pray before they embarked on the Iraqi roads. They wanted so desperately to shift the odds in their favor.

When the explosions happened and warriors were wounded, the spiritual questions became paramount. Their faith was being shattered little by little. They felt that God was somehow responsible. They felt abandoned by God. Those reared in church would doubt the teachings of God and faith they had heard since childhood. Their spiritual core values were being disrupted. They were experiencing spiritual trauma. It was a "burden" much like that carried by Habakkuk.

In his lament, Habakkuk does what we feel like doing, but most often hesitate. He goes directly to God with his concerns. Much like a trial lawyer, Habakkuk presents his case before the judge of the earth. Habakkuk is perplexed about God's apparent *indifference*, and the prophet is indignant. He is perplexed about God's apparent *inactivity*, and the prophet is incensed. He is perplexed about God's apparent *inconsistencies*, and the prophet is enraged.

The pain of unanswered questions is a burden that is sometimes difficult to carry. A family in my church community encountered a devastating tragedy. Their children were very involved in the church youth groups. One rainy day tragedy struck. Their oldest son was driving when his car began to hydroplane, and it was hit by another car. He was trapped inside and tragically killed. The questions were heard immediately: "Why?" "Why, God?" and "How could God allow this to happen to one so dedicated to his Christian faith and a witness to youth of all ages?" Even among those who quickly give the standard answers to such tragedies, there were signs of intense spiritual struggle with this apparent meaningless wreck. Some vocalized their questions, fearing criticism for doing so. Some put on the "all is well" face and pretended that God needed a youthful angel in heaven while denying the reality of their questions and refusing to entertain any doubts of faith. I returned once again with a saddened and burdened soul to Habakkuk with my unanswered questions.

For us to fully understand Habakkuk's burden, we need to look at the content of his prayers. The first petition of the prophet in verses 1–4 is a prayer of lament as the prophet shares his perplexity and pain to God. He is also presenting the predicament of the righteous in the nation.

> O Lord, how long shall I cry,
> and you will not hear?
> Even cry out to You, "Violence!"
> And you will not save.

Why do you show me iniquity,
And cause me to see trouble?
For plundering and violence are before me;
There is strife, and contention arises.
Therefore, the law is powerless,
And justice never goes forth.
For the wicked surround the righteous;
Therefore perverse judgment proceeds.

Habakkuk questions God's apparent *indifference*. There had been a great problem in the land, a lot of violence, and so Habakkuk says, "I'm going to pray about it." And he prays and he prays and he prays a little more, and there doesn't seem to be an answer. Rather than the situation getting better, it seems to get worse. And he's saying, "God, how long am I going to have to cry to you?" In Verse 2, he uses the word *cry* twice. The first word *cry* means a cry like a plea for help, but the second word *cry* is a different Hebrew word which means a shout or a scream. He's quit asking. He starts shouting at God as if he thinks God is deaf. "God! Why don't you do something?" I mean, he's angry. He's screaming aloud. He's pleading to God for help. But it seems like the heavens are silent.

Habakkuk dared to question the faith of his ancestors that he had learned since childhood. He understood the popular theology of his religious life; however, the traditional theological answers were not very helpful in the face of human suffering. He presented his protests to God because he was genuinely confused by the situation in Judah where evil was becoming progressively worse, the righteous were suffering and God was apparently apathetic.

I have been there. I have been to the place where I cried out and almost started to shout at God—a place where I really wanted to argue with God a little bit. I was mad at God. I would say, "God, why don't you do something? Why are you silent? Don't you care about what is happening?" There sometimes doesn't seem to be an answer. And I say, "Lord, how long am I going to have to pray about this?"

Remember the story in the gospels when Jesus was on the boat crossing the Sea of Galilee with some of his disciples. Suddenly a storm arose and waves beat against the boat. The disciples recognized that they were in danger and began to panic. They awakened Jesus and asked, "Master, don't you care that we perish?" They were accusing Jesus of indifference.

I have pondered and prayed, "God, don't you care about my problems, my pain, my situation, my suffering? God, don't you care?" The assumption is that if He did care, then He would intervene and change the circumstances and calm the seas.

Every day, on every continent of the world, God is accused of being indifferent. Terrible tragedies are replayed on our television sets, and people wonder, "Where is God? Doesn't God care about the earth? Why does God allow such atrocities?" Family and personal crises prompt similar questions about the compassion of God. Many diverse answers are provided in the sincere attempt to help people overcome their grief and their pain. But the answers usually fall short of helping heal the emotional and spiritual trauma. Something more than easy and empty answers is needed.

The second thing that Habakkuk complains about is God's apparent *inactivity*. It just seems to the prophet that God is up there with his arms folded and He's not doing a single thing about the situation in the world. In verse 3 Habakkuk asks, "Why do You show me iniquity, and cause me to see trouble? For plundering and violence are before me: There is strife and contention arises. Therefore the law is powerless, and justice never goes forth: For the wicked surround the righteous; therefore perverse judgment proceeds."

Everywhere the prophet looks, there is violence, trouble, robbery, and perverseness. "Habakkuk complained to God that the prophet dwelt in the midst of a people without moral restraints or abiding values" (Baily and Barker, p. 298). As a result, the authoritative law of God has fallen into disrespect—that which is designed to be the heart of the political, religious, and domestic life is "numbed" (could even say "quieted") and justice is corrupted. The devout followers of God are oppressed. Sounds familiar?

Habakkuk is saying, "Lord, haven't You noticed lately? Lord, haven't You looked down here? This world is in a mess, and there's violence, evil and trouble everywhere." Habakkuk says, "Lord, where are You? Don't You care? Why don't You do something about the desperate situation in our land?" It is almost like Habakkuk is accusing God of paralysis. "Surely, if you could, you would do something. What's the problem, God?"

Life sometimes throws us curves and we walk the same uneven terrain as Habakkuk? We wonder what could be stopping God from intervention. If He is the omnipotent, the all-powerful One, then surely He would help us, deliver us, heal us—do for us what we want and need. Surely, He would. All the time people ask me, "Why, Chaplain, doesn't God do something about this?" or "Why, Chaplain, didn't God intervene and stop this from happening?" Behind these soul-wrenching questions is the underlying thought of Habakkuk. Perhaps God is far removed from our personal or national concerns. Perhaps God simply chooses not to get involved. "But why?"

The third aspect of his burden was God's apparent *inconsistencies*. You see, God finally does respond to Habakkuk (verses 5–11).

> Look among the nations, and watch.
> Be utterly astounded!
> For I will work a work in your days
> Which you would not believe, though it were
>   told you.
> For indeed I am raising up the Chaldeans,
> A bitter and hasty nation
> Which marches through the breadth of the earth,
> To possess the dwelling places that are not theirs.
> They are terrible and dreadful:
> Their judgment and their dignity proceed from
>   themselves.
>
> Their horses also are swifter than leopards,
> And more fierce than evening wolves.

Their chargers charge ahead;
Their cavalry comes from afar
They fly as the eagle that hastens to eat.
They all come for violence;
Their faces are set like the east wind.
They gather captives like sand.
They scoff at kings,
And princes are scorned by them.
They deride every stronghold,
For they heap up earthen mounds and seize it.
Then his mind changes, and he transgresses;
He commits offense,
Ascribing this power to his god.

Though God answers the prophet, Habakkuk doesn't like what he hears. God says, "All right. You want to know what I'm doing. You don't think I'm doing anything? 'Look…and watch' and you will see. I'll tell you what I'm going to do. It's going to get worse. As a matter of fact, Habakkuk, I'm right now raising up a nation, the Chaldeans and their army is going to come. They're 'bitter,' that is, they're very cruel, and they're very 'swift.' They're going to march across the land of Israel, and they're going to take this place, and you're not going to be able to stop it. Their hunger is 'more fierce than evening wolves' which have not eaten all day. They come from afar to inflict violence. No king or prince or military stronghold will slow them down."

Wow! What an answer! Sure enough, Habakkuk didn't and couldn't believe what he was hearing. He was crying out because of the violence and trouble in the land and when God answers He states that even more trouble and violence is on its way. Habakkuk has prayed about how bad things are in his country and God states that things are going to get worse. Habakkuk asks, "Why do I see so much trouble and perverted justice?" And God states that He will see more contention and destruction. God's answer promises more of the same. Habakkuk is even more confused and complains even louder.

He had presented his case before God; the answer was not what he expected or wanted either for himself or for his country. The burden of his perplexity began to grow heavier. The only way to discharge the weight of his burden was to go back to God with his confusion of mind and crisis of faith. That is always the best and wisest course for troubled souls in trauma.

I have used a technique in counselling that has been very helpful to people experiencing the trauma of unanswered questions. Finding it extremely difficult to verbalize their pain, I have invited them to write a personal letter to God. This "Dear God" letter is intended to help them get in touch with their deepest feelings. Many have reported that it was awkward at first, but as they worked at it and continued the process, it opened up the soul. For many of these Marines and Sailors and their families, this was their first experience with personal, private prayer. They had confessed that they only recited prayers from their faith tradition and found it uncomfortable talking to God as one would another person. Putting the prayer on paper really helped remove this block. They were learning to pray for the first time in their lives. I invited them to bring their written prayer to a follow-up counseling session for discussion. I would ask them to read their "paper prayer" to God out loud. The emotional release was instantly evident as they shared their deepest concerns with God. These have been some of the most heartfelt and honest prayers I have ever heard. Rarely could I resist weeping with them.

Even among those who had been Christian for a long time and for whom prayer was as natural as breathing, the pain of unanswered questions slowed and stalled their prayer life, and they wanted and needed a jump start to help them pray. Their fierce anger and frustration with the events that God allowed to occur in their lives hindered their feeble attempts at prayer. Writing out their prayers and reading them to God unlocked many of the emotional blocks and unleashed suppressed pain and perplexity.

Habakkuk put his prayer on paper (paper equivalent at least). He did not give up on God. Sure, he questioned, but He went to God with his questions. He believed that God could change things.

If God did not, He believed that there had to be a reason, and so he wanted understanding of God's purpose. Habakkuk was not complaining for the sake of complaining. He was not engaged in self-pity. He prayed to understand, so he could help the righteous in the nation to understand. Baily and Barker have noted:

> He refused to have simply a faith of the fathers that he received without reflection. He refused to have a God of the fathers whose actions could be predicted or else must be accepted as correct without further investigation. Habakkuk insisted upon confronting God face to face and asking God the hard questions of life. He was not satisfied until answers came and dialog ensued. Only when he had wrestled in conversation with God and created a faith understanding of his own did he present a message to the public. (p. 254)

So Habakkuk continues to present his case before the Almighty with an expanded complaint. He presents his reasoned argument in verses 12–17.

> Are You not from everlasting,
> O Lord my God, my Holy One?
> We shall not die.
> O Lord, You have appointed them for judgment;
> O Rock, You have marked them for correction.
> You are of purer eyes than to behold evil,
> And cannot look on wickedness.
> Why do You look on those who deal treacherously,
> And hold Your tongue when the wicked devours
> A person more righteous than he?
> O Lord my God, my Holy One?
> We shall not die.

Why do You make men like fish of the sea,
Like creeping things that have no ruler over
    them?
They take up all of them with a hook,
They catch them in their net,
And gather them in their dragnet.
Therefore they rejoice and are glad.
Therefore they sacrifice to their net,
And burn incense to their dragnet;
Because by them their share is sumptuous
And their food plentiful.
Shall they therefore empty their net,
And continue to slay nations without pity?

I will paraphrase Habakkuk's argument. "Are You not from everlasting, O Lord?" In other words, "Lord, You didn't just get here yesterday. You should know what You are doing. Surely, You have given some thought to this decision. Lord, You've got it all mixed up. It's not Israel that needs to be punished. You are holy, so you must mean that the evil invaders are marked for your judgment. Not us, Lord! You're picking on the wrong crowd." And then he gives his rationale in Verse 13 (paraphrase):

> God, your plan is inconsistent. When I ask
> You to do something about the violence in our
> land, and ask You to do something about the
> crime in our land, and ask You to do something
> about the sin and the sickness in our land, and to
> do something for Your people and the suffering
> of the righteous, You tell me that You're going to
> bring the Babylonians to invade us. Now, God,
> that doesn't make sense! How can You do that?
> I mean, God, we're bad, but we're not as bad as
> they are. How can You use the wicked to devour

the man that is more righteous than he is? Now,
God, that is absolutely absurd.

Habakkuk could appreciate the fact that the wicked in Judah
who despised and disobeyed the Law of God deserved God's judgment. But he could not understand why God's retribution would
be at the hands of a people and nation whose god was their own
arrogance and army. Why would the "holy one" permit the heathen
warriors to humiliate God's people and harvest them like fish in a
net? The righteous in the land would also suffer at the hands of these
evil invaders. Why would a good and great God allow his people to
suffer such malice, misfortune, and misery?

How many times have we used or heard this argument? "Now,
look, God, wait a minute. We're bad. I'll admit we've sinned, but they
are worse than we are!" Why do we see those who profane the name
of god prospering and sincere and saintly people of God suffering?
Why do we see many who are evil, being promoted, being rewarded,
and being successful? I don't like it." And I want to tell you somebody
else who doesn't like it. Habakkuk doesn't like it. Habakkuk presents
a credible case.

I hear people talk about God a lot. When Marines and Sailors
would see the cross on my uniform, they always had something to
say about God and religion. I guess they thought it was expected of
them. The problems, pain, and perplexities that bring people to the
chaplain's office cause people to talk more about God. Many of these
people had not talked about God in a long time; some had never
talked about God. But here they were in the office of a chaplain, a
person of religious faith, and they concluded that they should use
"God talk."

It was often humorous listening to these young men and women
from the cities and towns of America attempting to find the acceptable words for talking to clergy. They usually knew why they had
come and what they wanted the chaplain to do for them (there are
those occasions when someone else sent them and they acted like they
have no idea why they are there), but they hesitated and struggled to

use the right words. Most often, I told them to simply say what is on their mind in the style with which they are most comfortable. Then, they would begin to feel free to open up and share their situation, often attempting to understand the reasons behind their personal predicaments and hoping to find some healing of their hurts. Their concerns and their questions were mostly legitimate, and they did not know to whom they could share their issues in confidence.

But too often, I hear questionable questions asked of God—questions that reflect a distorted view of God. He is often blamed for all kinds of evil. Yes, sometimes God allows and uses sorrow and tragedy to teach some greater good. God told Habakkuk that He would be using the evil Babylonians to discipline His chosen people. We know that learning and growing often occur through dark and difficult days as God helps with the process. However, we must be slow and cautious in blaming God as the cause of pain, the cause of disease, or the cause of tragedy. I have heard God blamed for killing babies, destroying marriages, causing miscarriages, causing car wrecks, causing abusive parents, and giving diseases. People's assumptions about God and His activity in the world can present serious obstacles to their faith formation. I have sat and listened to people who have so much unresolved anger toward God because they were at some time led to believe that God was the cause of every tragedy in their life. I am convinced that Christians in general and ministers in particular need to be more cautious and correct in expounding on the providence of God.

I have heard those with lung cancer question God when in fact, they had spent most of their lives smoking cancer-causing cigarettes. One patient I visited regularly complained about her asthma and wondered why God would not heal her, but at every opportunity she would sneak to the smoking area. I have also heard obese people question heart attacks, back problems, and other maladies related to being overweight. Once I heard a man question God because he was losing his foot to diabetes when he admitted that he was not eating the proper diabetic foods. Christians often seriously question God when they, themselves, are partly to blame for their circumstances.

I was once called to visit a home where a child had tragically drowned. Upon seeing me, the mother began hysterically asking "Why did God take my child?" I immediately thought to myself that God did not drown her child. The tragedy occurred the toddler had been left untended in a pool area. But all too often, God gets blamed and the goodness of God is questioned. However, I knew that she needed to express her grief, and even if I had to take the brunt of the attack, then I would. Her anger toward God was not legitimate, but it was authentic pain that needed expression.

I cannot remember the number of times that I have been yelled at and even slapped by people who were in dire distress due to a loss and they took their anger at God out on me as His representative. I sat with one family for hours as the director of Pastoral Care, Naval Hospital, Camp Lejeune, North Carolina, as they considered the doctor's opinion about removing life support. They were Christians and they argued about usurping God's prerogative to take life and whether God may yet heal their son and grandson. In their heated exchange, they began to take their anger out on me. I represented faith and God and right then they were struggling with faith and with anger toward God. They raised their voices; they began to yell; they bombarded me with questions about God and why. One lady was hysterical and began to slap my chest harder and harder until a son restrained her. They were convinced that God put him into this condition. "Why did God do this? What did he do so wrong to deserve this?" Now, their questions were questionable. Their anger was misdirected, but they needed to vent their fear, confusion, and terrible, raw pain. I was not there to defend God. I was there to be a positive, comforting presence.

In the biblical story of Job, he is visited by "friends" after his unspeakable series of tragedies. Kushner, in his classic work, *When Bad Things Happen to Good People*, observes,

> What Job needed from his friends—what he was really asking for when he said, "Why is God doing this to me?"—was not theology

but sympathy. He did not really want them to explain God to him, and he certainly did not want them to show him where his theology was faulty. He wanted them to tell him that he was in fact a good person, and that the things that were happening to him were terribly tragic and unfair. But the friends got so bogged down talking about God that they almost forgot about Job, except to tell him that he must have done something awful to deserve this fate at the hands of a righteous God. (p. 86)

My first funeral as a navy chaplain was for a young sailor who had died from injuries sustained during a car wreck. Members of the ship's crew were asking "why" God would take such a young life with so much potential. Many of them were seriously questioning God. I used the opportunity to speak to risky behaviors and immature actions that were the real cause. This young man was driving with alcohol in his system, at night and above the speed limit to get back to the ship before his leave had expired. So how could anyone blame God?

Though some questions of God may be questionable, the pain is real and the anger is legitimate. I can relate. Suffering from post-traumatic stress is common to war veterans. Blaming God for it may be a questionable question but I did just that. I was at the high point of my navy career. I had achieved the rank of navy captain. I dreamed of this time when I could mentor other chaplains. Yet my personal suffering of post-traumatic stress limited my involvement in the lives of others. I was just trying to stay afloat myself. When we had staff meetings and the door was closed, I felt immediate panic. I felt like I did in the back of a Humvee traveling the dangerous roads of Iraq or strapped inside a helicopter flying in the darkened skies all across western Iraq. I could not escape the feelings and the panic that set in. I was the leader but I felt out of control. I was very astute at hiding my feelings and few knew what I was experiencing. When helicopters flew over our base, I immediately felt like I was in Iraq with incoming wounded. When I heard the Marine artillery, I immediately felt the same emotions I felt in Iraq during outgoing or incoming fire. I could not escape these responses to sound and place. I was mad at God. Though my anger toward God was not legitimate, my anguish of soul was authentic. "Why now in my career? Why, God?"

My whole life was being affected. I could no longer go to a movie theatre unless we went very early so that I could get an end seat. I could only sit at the back of the church and on an end seat, which meant arriving early. I felt extreme anxiety at restaurants and in large groups. I suffered nightmares. Many times I fell out of the bed during a bad night and hit my head or shoulder or ribs on the floor. My sleep was always disturbed. The images of the wounded and dying Marines crossed my mind too many times. The counseling I had done with combat Marines caused its own anguish. Their experiences were in my thoughts and dreams. Counseling Mortuary Affairs Marines who described in detail their task of collecting the bodies and body parts of our Marines after explosions left indelible images in my mind. Visiting our wounded with missing legs and arms, deformed faces, and indescribable pain only contributed to my pain and my questions to God. Yes, my questions of God and anger toward God may not have been legitimate but they were real and painful and I had to express them to God. I was mad at God. "Why, God?"

One of my chaplains in Iraq had his office and chapel take a direct hit from a mortar round. Fortunately, no one was in the building at the time. The damage was extensive. I visited the camp sometime later and the shock was very evident. Seeing the destruction was a constant reminder to them about what could happen at any time. The chaplain continues to face his traumatized spirit and post-traumatic stress.

Habakkuk's perplexity was justified. There are situations in life that cause painful perplexity and we, like Habakkuk, legitimately cry out to God needing answers to our questions. There are also times when we shout to God in frustration and fury and though the reasons may be questionable, the pain is just as real and the need for God's grace and strength is needed the same.

Habakkuk had legitimate questions that tormented his soul. He took his questions to God in prayer.

Stained Glass

Fractured by tragedy.
Pieces, strewn by shocking circumstance,
Fallen still in thunderous silence of consequence.
Shards gleaned by the Master's hand,
Which bled and bleeds still for our pain—
We surrender to His arranging.
Our faith is breath taken while we wait.
Healing stirs, then warms
As light glows through seamed fragments,
And we behold a stained-glass portrait of His love.
(Milliner, *Pearl Haven: By the Sea*)

CHAPTER 2

The Perception of the Prophet

Waiting and Listening

Habakkuk presented his complaints to God. Honestly and openly, he shared the deepest questions of his soul. Now, it was time to listen to God. Habakkuk had spoken; now, he waited to receive the answer from God.

Habakkuk's Visit to the Watchtower

Chapter 2 begins with the prophet's going to his personal place of solitude. Habakkuk chooses to separate himself from others and to wait for God to address his rebuttal. His visit to the watchtower—his personal, private place of solitude—is to listen to God.

> I will stand my watch
> And set myself on the rampart,
> And watch to see what He will say to me,
> And what I will answer when I am corrected.
> (Habakkuk 2:1)

Most of our lives are characterized by busyness and rushing, by frenzied and feverish activity and its associated stress. When we complete the day's work, we often have an evening of responsibilities. So much movement, so many demands upon us, so many pressures. There are Monday things to do, Tuesday things to do, Wednesday requirements to meet and so on throughout the week. Sometimes it appears that our lives are being dictated by the clock and the calendar. We are acutely sensitive to being on time and to not wasting time, and yet, our chief complaint is that we never have enough time. This feeling of rush, hurry, work, and anxiety penetrates to the inner being of our spirit.

I shall never forget my father's scream every time I came to a stop sign when learning to drive. "Son, come to a complete stop!" I know my son Jonathan can remember all the times I said to him, "Son, come to a complete stop." Well, traveling familiar roads each day, I find myself slowing down at many stop signs, but not stopping. I am sure that many of you do the same. It describes our day, doesn't it? Most of us just find it too difficult to stop. Yet that is what we need to do most of all. Doesn't the Bible say that God stopped on the seventh day and sanctified it as a day of rest? Didn't Jesus intentionally separate himself time and time again from the crowds and from his own followers to find a place of solitude and silence? Jesus came to a complete stop—he needed to, and so do we.

Attending worship each week helps; it is a good "speed bump" to slow us down. But we learn from Habakkuk that God's answers to our concerns often come to those who wait in solitude and silence in their personal watchtower. Habakkuk left the maddening crowds. It is also imperative that we put on the brakes, pull over, and park. Our sanity sometimes demands it; our spirituality always requires it. I heard one preacher say, "If we don't come apart (prayer), we will come apart." "Be still and know that I am God" is revelation for the people of God. Going to our watchtower to hear from God is the key to spiritual renewal.

The particular place that we choose is not as important as the decision to seek solitude and silence. I know people who walk, some who run, some who stroll on the beach, those who drive on rural roads with little or no traffic, others who go to a church building, and those who choose a room in their own house. I like to cycle outside for long miles and use the time to reflect and pray. Whatever place we select for personal prayer becomes our soul's sanctuary as we seek God.

Solitude, stillness, and silence stand in contrast with our culture that expects action and activity always. Some equate stopping and stillness to laziness, lack of purpose and initiative. But the sheer number of books and articles being written on burnout today suggest that the Western culture has gone too far in the fast lane. Our marriages, our families, our communities and nation are showing evidence of our failure to feed the spirit.

While the director of Pastoral Care at Naval Hospital Camp Lejeune, I talked often with patients who confessed, "Chaplain, I couldn't stop, I wouldn't stop, so I guess that God had to stop me. I know that this illness will help me to focus on what is really important in life." This was their personal revelation. They would readily admit that they had become so swamped in the mundane that they lost their way; they lost sight of what is truly important, what is most meaningful and what has ultimate value. They had become victims of the modern culture, and their souls were suffering serious starvation.

"Yes," I would often reply. "Perhaps some of our personal storms are vehicles of revelation. Perhaps, God cares enough to use any means to help us evaluate our lives and to realize what is most important." As authors Gall et al. observe, "If a higher power is perceived to be at work in a stressful event, then the event may be viewed as an opportunity to learn something that the higher power is trying to teach. The event may also serve as a 'wake-up call' to take stock of life and rearrange priorities" (p. 95–96). If we listen carefully, we may hear God say to us, "Come to a complete stop." God may be heard saying to us, "Take the time to focus on the spiritual; make the time, choose the place, and come apart to pray." Psychologist Jonathan Haidt in his book *The happiness hypothesis: finding modern truth in ancient wisdom* observes, "Adversity may be necessary for growth because it forces you to stop speeding along the road of life, allowing you to notice the paths that were branching off all along, and to think about where you really want to end up" (p. 144). Habakkuk stopped, waited for God and was pleasantly surprised.

The immortal words of Isaiah the prophet express it clearly. The people were questioning the apparent absence of God: "Why do you say, O Jacob, And speak, O Israel: 'My way is hidden from the Lord, and my just claim is passed over by my God'?" They were seriously concerned that God was not giving sufficient attention to their plight and prayers. However, the prophet received a revelation for the people which have been a spiritual comfort to Christians through the centuries:

> Have you not known? Have you not heard?
> The everlasting God, the Lord, the Creator of the
> ends of the earth,
> Neither faints nor is weary.
> His understanding is unsearchable.
> He gives power to the weak,
> And to those who have no might,
> He increases strength.
> Even the youths shall faint and be weary.
> And the young men shall utterly fall.
> But those who wait on the Lord
> Shall renew their strength;
> They shall mount up with winds like eagles,
> They shall run and not be weary,
> They shall walk and not faint. (Isaiah 40: 27–31)

It cannot be stated any more succinctly and clearly—our spiritual strength is directly related to waiting on God. I am convinced that the "waiting" the prophet Isaiah had in mind is the "waiting" practiced by Habakkuk after his complaint was presented to God. To "wait on the Lord" means to step into our individual place of solitude and silence and be still before God. Mysterious and miraculous transformations take place in the presence of God—one's strength is renewed for the long haul. Habakkuk will soon find out for himself.

Observe that Isaiah connects waiting on God with renewal of strength like eagles that use the winds to go high and fast. This renewal helps us to run and not grow exhausted and to walk and not faint. It is strength to help us overcome the overwhelming questions and pain. It is for those who wait on God.

Habakkuk stepped aside from the public arena to his private sanctuary to meet God. The British philosopher James Martineau noted,

> Let any man go into silence: strip himself of all Pretense, and selfishness and sensuality, and sluggishness of soul; lift off thought after thought, passion after passion till he reaches the inmost depth of all; and it will be strange if he or does not feel the Eternal presence as close upon his soul, as the breeze upon the brow. (Public Quotes)

Habakkuk came to his place of solitude and silence with his questions, but his real quest was God himself. Stillness and silence encourage deep reflection. In these quiet moments, we discover God's purposes. Our fears and anxieties melt away, and stress is reduced. Our life is renewed to see our circumstances in God's revealing light.

In his place of solitude and silence, the prophet perceived the revelation of God. Habakkuk had to turn off the noise of the world and "the distracting electronics" to hear the voice of the divine. He had to quiet his mind from its tormenting questions and focus entirely upon God. His quest was not to experience some spiritual high or merely to escape the pressures of life with meditative thought. He went to his watchtower with one clear purpose—to wait for God. Habakkuk believed, perhaps because of past experiences, that when he stepped aside from all distractions, his soul could sense God's presence and perceive God's word for him.

*Habakkuk had to turn off the noise of the
world to hear the voice of the divine.*

Meditation and various spiritual exercises borrowed from Eastern religions grow increasingly popular in the West. Books, conferences, and websites are devoted to teaching the value of different forms of yoga and other meditative practices. While their benefit has been verified by the medical community as a means to reduce anxiety, to heal the body and to maximize coping skills, Habakkuk teaches a more valuable purpose. The body may heal more quickly and the mind become less troubled, but a person can be left with an inescapable emptiness of the spirit. The unanswered questions can continue to call for answers. The spiritual struggle to understand the reason, the why, can remain a burden upon the spirit. Something more is needed. Though it can be found in the place of solitude, stillness, and silence, it is not the silence and its accompanying relaxation that is the answer. If a distressed person is simply satisfied with the positive feelings experienced in solitude, he/she can miss the spiritual reflection and renewal that is most needed and rewarding.

Habakkuk sets an example for us to emulate. He takes the initiative to isolate himself. Habakkuk had presented his petitions to God in prayer. His deepest concerns were shared with God. His soul was laid bare before God. He was not pleased with the answers that he had received from God. So now he simply seeks to listen.

Much too often, prayer and meditative silence are confused. Habakkuk had previously presented his petitions before God in prayer. Now, he retires to a quiet place to simply listen. There is no other agenda; his only purpose is to open his soul to God.

I have found prayer to be therapeutic—emotionally, mentally, and spiritually. The time devoted to soul silence is an aspect of prayer that is also vitally important. Like the prophet, we remove ourselves from others and go to a quiet place of solitude to intentionally listen to God. We simply sit or stand or even lie in our place of solitude, engaging in the sounds of silence and listening for a word from God. Kushner observes:

> In your desperation, you opened your heart in prayer, and what happened? You didn't get a miracle to avert a tragedy. But you discovered people around you, and God beside you, and a strength within you to help you survive the tragedy. I offer that as an example of a prayer being answered. (p. 131)

As Habakkuk experienced, God comes to those who seek him.

It is worth noting again that the prophet expected a form of rebuttal or retribution from God. In chapter 2 verse 1, he states that he would visit his watchtower and "watch to see what He will say to me, and what I will answer when I am corrected." He had complained to God about His plans and in an angry tone questioned God's reasoning and judgment. He appears justified in expecting some form of reprisal.

I was a young chaplain serving with a Marine group in Hawaii. I had voiced my concerns and objections to the commanding officer's guidance to company commanders about unit run failures to my senior chaplain. Each company had to report to the headquarters how many of their Marines had fallen out of the unit's weekly three-mile run. None of the young officers wanted to submit any numbers from their company. Therefore, on unit runs I witnessed a lot of verbal abuse by leaders upon those having difficulty keeping up. On one particular run, I watched as various Marines yelled at a female trying her best to keep up but not maintaining the pace. The remarks went beyond encouragement. I was embarrassed at what I was hearing and seeing. Then, I saw several motivated Marines begin to push her to keep her going.

The pushing became more pronounced as she slowed. I was angry and determined that I would complain even louder. I discovered at the end of the run that the young lady had fallen out and passed out and an ambulance was called to pick her up. I was livid. Upon returning to the headquarters building, I went directly to the commanding officer of the unit. I accosted him in the hallway and expressed in an angry tone my deepest concerns with his policy. I stated that this woman might die, and it would be his fault. If you know anything about military protocol, then you know that I was on dangerous ground. The wise and experienced colonel told me to go take a shower and return in an hour to his office with my supervisory chaplain. As I left, the full impact of what I had just done hit me. "Did I really say those things to the colonel? O me! I am in serious trouble." When I finished my shower, I briefed my supervisory chaplain about what I had done. Though he agreed with my principles, he correctly advised that I had gone about it the wrong way. He went with me to meet with the colonel. I will never forget that meeting. The blind courage that I felt earlier was gone as I sat nervously in the office of this war veteran and highly respected leader. I waited for the ax to fall. His words were few, but firm. "Lee, I want my chaplains to tell me what they think. I value my chaplain's opinions. But your tone and manner in presenting you concerns were inappropriate. Is that understood?"

"Yes, sir," I responded quickly, expected more to follow.

"You are dismissed," he said. I departed and my supervisory chaplain remained behind to receive what I thought had to be the hammer.

I returned to my office and waited. My boss and first chaplain mentor and friend returned with a smile on his face. I was surprised to see the smile and hoped it was a happy smile. He explained to me that the colonel really did appreciate my forthrightness. He wants his chaplains to speak for the troops. He also said that he was unaware of the aggressive tactics used by some of his men and would meet with the company commanders to stop it immediately. I learned a valuable lesson from this Marine leader who could have punished me for my angry outbursts. He did not object to my anger or my questions. He was not upset that I questioned his policy. He wanted me to visit him and express any of my concerns, but to do so respectfully in the proper military manner. My chaplain supervisor could have held this against me, but he wanted it to be a learning experience for me. It was! His leadership and benevolent reaction was never forgotten.

To the surprise of the prophet Habakkuk, God did not rebuke him for his angry outbursts. The prophet was deeply concerned about his people and their suffering. He told God so. God responded to the perplexed prophet with a revelation of truth—not a rebuke of terror. Habakkuk was surprised, if not shocked. We learn from his experience that it is all right for us to go to the commanding officer of the entire world with what is on our mind without fear of reprisal.

> *God responded to the perplexed prophet*
> *with a revelation of truth—*
> *not a rebuke of terror.*

Habakkuk was not condemned for his accusations toward God and his argument with God because he talked to God in honest, sincere, and reverent prayer. He had serious questions about God's management of things and felt free to express them to God. But to Habakkuk, presenting his argument was not the essential issue. The prophet wanted God's response. His spiritual life needed God's response. The righteous in the land for whom he was speaking also needed a word from God.

Perspectives (what we want in life) are changed, priorities (what is most important) are changed, and persons (who we are and who we want to be) are transformed in the presence of God. Spiritual renewal takes place when we intentionally withdraw from worldly distractions and commune with God. Habakkuk discovered this truth during his time alone with God.

"Just Have Faith"

Faith is fundamental to a Christian's life. For most, their religious faith becomes the primary means of coping when disaster or tragedy strikes. A National Survey conducted by Schuster et al. (2001) shows that after the terrorist attacks of September 11, 2001, 90 percent of Americans turned to prayer, religious faith, or another form of spiritual activity in an effort to cope. When Piedmont, Alabama, was hit by a tornado that destroyed a local church filled with members and killing several children, including the pastor's four-year-old daughter, the survivors struggled intensely with their questions: "Why?" "Why a church?" "Why God?" "Why the children?" Though badly shaken by this crisis, the pastor and parishioners commented that while:

> Their faith is shaken, it is *not* the same as losing it. Events like this only strengthen our faith...Our *faith* is an anchor in a turbulent sea... Those who die inside a church will find the gates of heaven open wide.... As long as we have faith, we are strong. No matter how dark it is, if I have faith, I have a song in the night.... Our beliefs are trembled and bent, but they did *not* break.... There is no reason. Our faith is *not* determined by reason. Our faith is undergirded by belief, where there is no reason. (Meichenbaum, p. 545)

There are so many accounts of how those who endured traumatic events relied upon their religious faith and came out on the other side with thanksgiving and praise to God for His strength. Faith in God and the support of a community of faith can give Christians what they so desperately need in the time of crisis.

Studies indicate that Americans are a religious people. Pargament in his book *Spiritually Integrated Psychotherapy* offers the following statistics to show how central religion is in America.

- Over 90% of Americans believe in God or in a higher power.
- 60% belong to a local religious group.
- 60% think that religious matters are important or very important in how they conduct their lives.

- 40% attend religious services almost weekly or more.
- 80% are interested in "growing spiritually."

Pargament adds the following statistics:

- 30% of adults in US pray daily and 80% pray when faced with a serious problem or crisis.
- 64% report that they read the Bible or other inspirational literature on a regular basis.
- 70% believe in some form of afterlife.
- 45% report that they definitely believe in the devil and another 20% state they probably do.
- 43–60%of people who have emotional problems *turn first* to their clergy for help.

When crisis strikes, the majority of Americans turn to spiritual core values for support. Their faith becomes the bedrock of strength in their personal storms. Trusting in their faith in God, people are able to cope more effectively and many are able to turn the tragedy into a triumph of meaning and growth.

Several major studies have been conducted that demonstrate that people who use religious and spiritual coping skills show greater physical and emotional well-being (Pargament 2007). These include lower levels of depression and alcohol consumption, fewer somatic complains, fewer interpersonal problems, higher levels of life satisfaction, an overall improved coping ability and lower mortality. One's faith and connection to a religious community and participation in religious rituals give a person a sense of being loved and valued, despite a person's personal sense of being damaged, abused, and abandoned Placing one's faith in a merciful and loving God can enable a traumatized individual to preserve belief in a just world.

There are, however, those traumatic events which challenge our faith in God and undermine our entire belief system. Faith becomes problematic. Yes, "just have faith" usually works, but this time, it does not. "What now?"

During my developmental years as a Christian, I was unduly influenced by preachers and teachers who proclaimed "just have faith" theology to every problem solution. If one "just had more faith," then healing would occur. If one "just had more faith," then problems would be solved. If one "just had more faith," then money would flow in. If one "just had more faith," then all their marital difficulties would disappear. If one "just had more faith," then there would be no questions of God. I watched countless number of times as hurting people were told that the reason they continued to be sick and to suffer was their lack of faith. This only added to their burden; now, they were convinced that their failure to have faith caused their problems. I witnessed the spiritual flagellation (longer fasts and more prayers) as sincere Christians attempted to work hard to produce "more faith" that would make life free of problems. When the "more faith" did not result from their working to produce it, there was discouragement, self-abuse, and guilt. They blamed themselves for their suffering; they blamed themselves for the problems and pain of family members. If only they had "more faith," then everything would be all right. I soon discovered that there are Christians everywhere who have been influenced by this belief and hurt by its inadequacy to live up to its promise.

As a teenaged Christian, the "just have faith" teaching contributed to many personal, spiritual struggles. When problems did not disappear after sincere and serious prayer, I was convinced that something had to be wrong with me. I would engage in prolonged introspection to identify the sins which kept God from answering my prayers. There was more perplexity than peace. I allowed guilt rather than grace to rule in my heart. My perceived lack of faith caused great consternation; I believed that such lack of faith made me an inferior Christian. Thus, I was always asking for more "faith" instead of celebrating the grace I had received from God.

This "just have more faith" belief espoused by some popular, charismatic preachers today is hurting more people than it is helping. Yes, we all would like to think if only I could produce a stronger faith, then I could have all I want—health, happiness, and a host of extras—but this is not consistent with biblical revelation. Habakkuk was a prophet of God who suffered intense anguish of soul. Many, if not most of the prophets and preachers of Scripture, endured dark and difficult days. Their great faith in God did not exempt them from tragedies and suffering, or always deliver them from their troubles. Consider the sufferings of the apostle Paul described in 2 Corinthians:

> [I]n labors more abundant
> in stripes above measure
> in prisons more frequently,
> in deaths often.
> From the Jews five times I received forty stripes
> minus one.
> Three times I was beaten with rods;
> once I was stoned;
> three times I was shipwrecked
> a night and a day I have been in the deep;
> In journeys often,
> in perils of waters
> in perils of robbers
> in perils of my own countrymen,
> in perils of the Gentiles,
> in perils in the city,
> in perils in the wilderness,
> in perils in the sea,
> in perils among false brethren;
> in weariness and toil,
> in sleeplessness often,
> in hunger and thirst,
> in fastings often,
> in cold and nakedness
> besides the other things,

what comes upon me daily;
my deep concern for all the churches. (2
Corinthians 11:23–28)

Paul was not on a quest to possess "more faith" to escape these trials and tribulations. Paul expresses his personal quest: "This one thing I do… I press toward the goal for the prize of the upward call of God in Christ Jesus" (Philippians 3:13b, 14). Paul didn't want "more faith"; Paul wanted more of God. Habakkuk will ultimately show us that an encounter with God is what will help us not only endure our problems, but also rejoice in the midst of them. When we experience God, our problems, though present, seem minuscule.

Paul penned most of the New Testament letters. He established churches, groomed Christian leaders, and embraced non-Jews into the Christian family. His contributions to the early church are incalculable. Yet this giant of faith suffered such a horrendous blow to his faith so that he became depressed. In 2 Corinthians chapter 1 verse 8, Paul describes his condition like being pressed in a vice and pressured from all sides. It was more than he could handle, "above strength." He does not inform us what the problem was but he does denote its seriousness. It had buckled his emotional, mental, physical, and spiritual knees and he was in desperation. He thought he was to die. We learn that hard times and unmanageable crises come to all people of faith.

While I was a ship's chaplain, we were in Hawaii completing a visit when Hurricane Ewa made her way to the Hawaiian islands. An immediate call was issued to get underway so the ship would not be pier side during the storm. As we slowly navigated the channel, the winds reached tropical storm strength. Several of our antennae were damaged as we made our way to the open seas. I went topside to see how bad it was. I could not believe the size of the waves breaking upon the channel entrance. I thought to myself, "Are we going out there; can this ship survive such a storm?" This was my first storm on the sea, and I had some questions and fears that I needed addressed.

I walked up to the bridge and stood in the entrance and watched the well-trained and confident sailors doing their jobs. I saw the ship's commanding officer sitting relaxed in his captain's chair. I walked over to him and made a comment about the storm. I cannot remember a word he said, but I know that his demeanor, his absolute confidence in his crew and ship, and his positive outlook silenced all my fears. I was then able to go below and be available for others who were experiencing a storm of this magnitude for the first time and needing some reassurance. The difference in my outlook was the visit to the commanding officer. The storm did not subside. In fact, the entire night I was strapped in my bunk as we rolled and pitched in the heavy seas. Though my visit to the captain did not calm the storm, it calmed my anxious heart. Somewhat simplistic, I know, but I have discovered the same principle applies to the storms of life. When I visit God in prayer, the difficulties that challenge my coping resources may not disappear. The storm may continue to rage with awesome force, but I have been calmed and reassured in the presence of God. The visit to God changes my perception of my problems. They are not quite as big and awesome in the presence of God.

My experience has shown me that these visits to God increase my confidence and courage to face my problems and provide the insight and inspiration I need to solve my problems. The author of Psalm 42 experienced this truth. He confesses that "God is our refuge and strength, a very present help in trouble" (v. 1). God's presence is a place of protection and strength. A visit to God had reassured this writer. He is able to proclaim (vv. 2, 3):

> Therefore we will not fear,
> Though the earth be removed,
> And though the mountains be carried
> into the midst of the sea;
> Though its waters roar and be troubled,
> Though the mountains shake with its swelling.

These words express how I felt after my visit to the captain of this ship. "Though its waters roar and be troubled," I will not fear. The psalmist never said that his troubles would vanish, but rather "The Lord of hosts is with us; The God of Jacob is our refuge" (v. 7). And God responded to this writer saying, "Be still and know that I am God." Plainly, in prayer, the prophet came to understand that God was present with him as his sure source of safety and strength.

No Escape

There are those troubled times when we have had enough and want desperately to escape. We look around for a red, lighted Exit sign, but none is in sight. The trouble continues and the lack of an escape route causes us to panic.

While assigned to Marine Corps Air Station Yuma, I went with my unit Marines to the Arizona desert during a field training exercise. I was in a foxhole with a young Marine. We were positioned on top of a hill and canisters of tear gas were being thrown down at those approaching from below. Suddenly, the wind shifted and the gas came toward us. Immediately, I turned and put on my gas mask, but the Marine with me panicked as the gas settled into our hole. He jumped out and ran away, leaving his rifle in the hole. The feeling of having to escape overwhelmed him and he created more trouble for himself. This Marine learned a very important lesson after being seriously—and I mean seriously—reprimanded by his sergeant for departing his place of duty and leaving his rifle (and the chaplain) behind. Running is not the way to face your troubles.

I have counseled people who act in a similar fashion. In their attempt to escape their problems, they create more complications for themselves. They make rash, unreasoned decisions to escape what they perceive to be an insurmountable predicament. I have visited them in the hospital as they recover from a suicide attempt; I visited them in the brig (navy jail) as they face punishment for going on an unauthorized absence (leaving their unit without permission). Some decide to leave their marriages and families to escape the effort required to make marriage work; others quit jobs, leave one location for another, or leave one church for another; and others escape into themselves. Troubles, however, tend to follow us wherever we go and whatever we do. Eventually, we must learn to face our problems, whatever their nature, and deal with them.

Habakkuk shows us the better way. The prophet shows us how important it is for us to take our "burdens to the Lord." Sharing our burdens with God can lighten our load. The problems may then appear to be more manageable. Our confidence can increase and our desire to tackle the troubles we face can be renewed. Our questions may not be answered, but in the presence of God we become "battle ready." Then, we can return to the front lines of spiritual warfare. We are enabled to "walk and not faint" and "to run and not be weary" in spite of our intellectual inquisition of God.

Uncharted Problems

Have you ever felt like things in life have been going too well, and you had a strange suspicion that this was going to change? You knew intuitively that some problem was going to arise. "Things just can't continue going this well," you thought. Then one day, something totally unexpected happens: bad news, illness, disappointment, or some other crisis comes out of nowhere. Whether you are "ready or not," the problem comes into your life. Read the story of Job.

During my first six-month deployment as a ship's chaplain, we were training in the waters off Australia. Our mission was to anchor off shore and let the Marines onboard storm the beach. I was on the flight deck talking to some sailors when we felt a sudden and disturbing shake of the ship. Within minutes, we all knew that we had hit something and run aground. The attempt was made to move the ship and we were finally free of the ground. Word spread quickly about the ship that we had hit an "uncharted reef." We returned slowly to port in Australia for immediate repairs and steamed on to the Philippines for extensive repairs. The coral reef had done terrible damage to the ship. The morale among the crew was low as we all asked, "Why?" The ship had been excelling in all tests and training. We were sure to win the competition among the ships in our Group as the "best." And now this!

Uncharted and unexpected problems arise in our lives which can suddenly challenge all our resources—mental, emotional, physical, and spiritual. Sometimes they appear out of nowhere. "The timing is terrible! We don't need this now," we ponder. There are too many other things that require our time, attention, and energy. And now this!

We cannot help but ask "why?" "Why can't God at least control the timing of these things?" These unexpected problems often catch us unprepared. We question "why" these things are happening to us now. "God knows what my life is like, so why is He permitting this?" Habakkuk wonders the same. The righteous people are facing enough problems already, but God says to the prophet that worse is coming. He is seriously confused by all this, so he cries out to God for justification.

While stationed at Kaneohe Bay, Hawaii, I decided to take sailing lessons. I completed the course and invited my thirteen-year-old daughter and nine-year-old son to go with me on my first sailing adventure. We started out just fine until I decided to go around a small island in the bay. As we were sailing around, the wind picked up and started to blow us toward the shallow waters. I tried to put down my stabilizer, but it was broken. I felt absolutely helpless as the wind blew us toward the rocks. You can imagine what my children were saying. They were frightened, and they vocalized no confidence in my sailing abilities. Greatly embarrassed and disappointed, I faced reality—I needed help! I pulled down the sails and began to wave frantically at boaters who passed by. Finally, someone came to our rescue and pulled us back to the marina—to shore, to safety, and to stories to tell.

I have often reflected on this event as a lesson on life. We can be sailing along with good wind on a sunny day, when unexpectedly clouds appear in the sky, winds pick up speed, and we are caught in bad weather. There were no predictions of bad weather when I took my children sailing, but it came anyhow. Just like life. "Chaplain, I didn't expect this. What do I do? Chaplain, I don't understand why God allowed this to happen to us now. We have other problems we are trying to solve." "Chaplain, this caught us totally unprepared. I need help." Many more similar questions have been asked of me as unexpected problems arise and overwhelm people who are already troubled by other concerns. It's like "ready or not, here I come." And come they do. We wonder why. We question the timing.

God's Timing

When Habakkuk received the response from God, it was not a rebuttal as he expected, but a revelation he revered. This revelation from God is so important that the prophet is instructed to write it so plainly that those who run by can read it. No one is to miss this message. It was to be in large, bold print for all to read. We could even paraphrase for our day, "Place the answer on a billboard so that all the passersby can see and read it."

> Then the Lord answered me and said:
> Write the vision
> And make it plain on tablets,
> That he may run who reads it.
> For the vision is yet for an appointed time;
> But at the end it will speak, and it will not lie.
> Though it tarries, wait for it;
> Because it will surely come,
> It will not tarry. (Habakkuk 2:2, 3)

Requiring the prophet to write the vision down is significant because the writing gives the vision some permanence. This is not a temporary word, but a promise for all time. It is a promise we can count on. It is written in indelible ink we might say. There is to be no confusion as to the word of God to the prophet. This is a revelation for all times and circumstances. It will not fail!

God says to the prophet that the answer "will surely come, it will not tarry." The answer is on its way; however, it comes according to a different time schedule than ours. The revelation is coming according to God's timetable. Its arrival cannot be rushed. We must wait for it. Though it appears slow or delayed, it will eventually come. God's answer will come to all those who wait. As it is used here, *waiting* implies expectation and anticipation. One is to anticipate an answer. We are reminded that God's time runs on a different clock than ours. In time, and only God knows exactly when, we will know the answer. This is where faith must fill the gap. Until the time that God chooses to make known his purpose and plan for us, we are to be faithful.

The story of Joseph is one of the best examples of this truth (Genesis 37–50). A favorite son of his father Jacob, Joseph had special privileges. His ten brothers, however, did not think too much of his preferred status. When opportunity came, they sold him to foreign merchants and reported to their father that he had been brutally killed by a vicious beast. Betrayed by his brothers, he was carried to a foreign country away from family and home.

Joseph was subsequently sold to Potiphar in Egypt. Working as a slave for the house of Potiphar, Joseph attempted to make the best out of a bad situation. He worked hard and gained the trust and confidence of his master. Potiphar really liked Joseph, but so did Potiphar's wife. She sought to seduce the young, handsome Hebrew, but Joseph consistently resisted her sexual advances. The day came when she had enough of the refusals of this foreigner and she reported to her husband an attempted rape by his employee. Joseph was then sent to prison. Things went from bad to worse and I can only imagine the many questions that Joseph had for God.

While in prison, he used his gift of dream interpretation to explain the meaning of the dreams of Pharaoh's chief butler and baker. The interpretations were fulfilled as Joseph had predicted. Sometime later when the Pharaoh of Egypt was having a recurring dream and no one was able to give him a satisfying interpretation, his chief butler remembered the gift of the Hebrew in Potiphar's prison. Joseph was carried to interpret the dream of the Pharaoh of Egypt. His interpretation was most satisfying. Joseph had predicted seven years of full harvests followed by seven years of famine. His advice was to collect surplus in the bountiful years to have available for the years of drought. The Pharaoh gave to Joseph the responsibility of the project. Joseph went from being a prisoner in the house of Potiphar to becoming a prime minister in the house of Pharaoh.

During those years of famine, his family came to Egypt for food. Joseph was in the right place at the right time to provide for his family. He was able to see clearly the divine purpose in all that had transpired in his life. He told his repentant brothers, "And God sent me before you to preserve a posterity for you in the earth, and to save your lives by a great deliverance" (Genesis 45:7).

The years of disgrace were designed to get him into the palace. He saw the providence of God in all that had transpired in his life. All the troubles he had to encounter and suffering he endured was in God's overall plan for the provision and protection of his people. However, for Joseph it was a long wait before he could fully see the plan of God.

Perhaps, this is what is meant by God's word to Habakkuk. The answer will come eventually; it may be a while, but it will come at the appointed time. Sometimes we may be privileged to understand the reason and discover the meaning of our personal trials. Whether we receive a personal revelation or not, however, Habakkuk's message for us is clear. As we wait to understand, "the just shall live by his faith." The following poem makes this message clear.

The Divine Weaver

My life is but a weaving
Between my Lord and me;
I cannot choose the colours
He worketh steadily

Ofttimes He weaveth sorrow
And I in foolish pride,
Forget that He seeth the upper,
And I the under side.
Not till the loom is silent
And the shuttles cease to fly,
Shall God unroll the canvas
And explain the reason why.
The dark threads are as needful
In the Weaver's skillful hand,
As the threads of gold and silver
In the pattern He has planned.(Author Unknown)

I worked for two years for a very demanding, hard-core Marine. Our unit made weekly runs of three to eight miles. We would have a hike with full packs once a quarter from ten to fifteen miles. I reported to the Marine unit at forty-one years of age after a one-year educational program funded by the navy. I was not in the best shape of my life. But being a navy chaplain means that we run and hike with our units and endure the same hardships as they. Ten years earlier, I loved these exercises of "grit" and sought to prove to the Marines that a navy chaplain could keep up. But now, my body did not cooperate as before. Back and knee problems made this time most difficult.

I often prayed to God "why" did I get this particular unit? I talked with many of my chaplain friends, and they were not doing half of the running and hiking that we were required to do. On many of the ten- to twenty-mile hikes with full packs, as the sun would beat down upon us and the North Carolina humidity became unbearable, I would be angry at God. I complained about my suffering and wondered why I couldn't be on a comfortable ship? Why did I get this Marine leader? My questions continued as my body suffered more abuse and I was required to go to physical therapy for relief and recuperation.

The answer did not come. I completed my assignment and moved on. Four years later, I received an e-mail from a friend who forwarded to me an e-mail he had received from the Marine leader who had caused me such trouble and trauma (physical and mental). In this e-mail, he stated that he had suffered from clinical depression and had to be hospitalized. He remarked that "his favorite chaplain" (I could not believe those words) saved his life. When contemplating suicide, he remembered one of my lectures on suicide prevention. He sought professional help and was recovering from his mental nightmare. Could this be the reason "why" I had to endure the physical and mental challenges of those years? Maybe so! Sometimes, we may have to wait a long time to understand the reason; sometimes, we may not understand in this life.

The Righteous Shall Live By Faith

God's answer to Habakkuk appears, on first reading, to support the "just have faith" theology. God tells Habakkuk that "the just shall live by faith." The primary difference, however, is that God never tells the prophet that the troubles will end. In fact, in spite of faith, God informs Habakkuk that his world will be turned upside down. Worse is coming. The faith that the righteous need is not to escape the trouble, but to endure the trouble and to enrich the trouble with the presence of God. Paul in Romans 8:35–39 supports this idea:

Who shall separate us from the love of Christ?
Shall tribulation, or distress, or persecution, or
famine, or nakedness, or peril, or sword?
As it is written:
'For Your sake we are killed all day long;
We are accounted as sheep for the slaughter.'
Yet in all these things we are more than
conquerors through Him who loved us.
For I am persuaded that neither death nor life,
nor angels nor principalities nor powers,

nor things present nor things to come,
nor height nor depth, nor any other created
thing,
shall be able to separate us from the love of God
which is in Christ Jesus our Lord.

Paul makes it clear that Christians can be "more than conquerors" in spite of the hardships and heartaches that life may heap upon them. He covers about every possible scenario one may encounter in life. "Tribulation, distress, persecution, famine, nakedness, peril, and sword" cover the wide gamut of problems. Paul wants it to be clear that whatever the struggle or suffering, God can keep the believer in His love. He was so convinced that he added "neither death or life, nor angels, nor principalities, nor powers, nor things present, nor things to come, nor height nor depth, nor any other created thing." Is there anything else? Yet he confidently states that in the midst of any and all of these circumstances we can be "more than conquerors." We can be overcomers—not merely survivors. Absolutely nothing, not our questions, not our anger toward God or others, no, nothing can separate us from God's love. This is faith. It is a gift of God. Habakkuk will get there eventually.

To fully understand what God is saying to Habakkuk, we need to look carefully at this phrase, "the just shall live by faith"—three words in Hebrew, and each one significant (Habakkuk 2:4). First, "the just" (Hebrew, *tsaddik*), is translated *righteous ones*. The word does not denote saintly qualities as we would expect. It is a rather a legal term which means that this person has been legally declared right. It likely refers to those who have dedicated themselves to obeying the law of God. God has declared them to be righteous.

The writer of Psalm 1 makes a sharp contrast between the righteous and the wicked, and it aids in our understanding of the terms. The "blessed" (Hebrew, *'ashre*) or happy person is one who is guided by the law of God. This person shall be like a firmly rooted, flourishing, and fruitful tree. This person is among the righteous (v. 6) whose way is known by God.

The wicked are those who do not make any serious effort to keep God's law and who are content in their rebellious living. He uses three distinct Hebrew words to describe the nature of the wicked. The ungodly (Hebrew, *rasha'*) are those who choose their own way and their lives become distorted and disjointed—out of harmony with God's purpose; the sinners (Hebrew, *hatta'*) are those who decide to disobey the law of God and despise his commandments; the scoffers (Hebrew, *letsim*) are those who scorn religious faith.

The righteous, then, are those who reject the council of the ungodly, but rather choose to abide by the commandments of God. They refuse to follow the course of sinners, but rather choose commitment to the will and way of God. The righteous reject the companionship of the scoffers, but rather choose the company of the faithful. Therefore, the righteous are those who have decided to regulate their conduct by the law of God; the law of God is their source of joy and they meditate on it frequently (Psalm 1). The "righteous shall live by faith."

> *The righteous are those who have decided to regulate their conduct by the law of God; the law of God is their source of joy and they meditate on it frequently. The righteous shall live by faith.*

In Habakkuk 2:4, the second Hebrew word in this most important phrase, "the righteous shall live by faith," is translated "live." Those who regulate their lives by the law of God shall live. In Hebrew thought "to live" means much more than mere breathing enough to sustain life. Martin-Achard in *From Death to Life* defines the Hebrew meaning of life:

> Thus life is primarily a force; indeed it is precisely what the expression 'vital force' brings to our minds; its nature is to express itself, to act, to move, to fulfil itself; therefore it involves mobility, spontaneity, and development; it must grow,

flourish, and accomplish its end; the absence of movement, freedom, or future is tantamount to its negation. (p. 5)

Returning to the metaphor in Psalm 1, to live is to be the tree planted by the waters bearing its fruit in season. It is fully productive. It has what it needs for growth and maturity. Firmly rooted. Flourishing. Fruit-filled.

In these times of distress, the person is usually not experiencing the fullness of life. He wants to enjoy life and hopes to experience a flourishing future, but he feels that his whole being is being threatened. The suffering person is seeking to regain his life. His perplexity has disrupted the harmony of his life; the suffering person's sense of *shalom* has been shaken.

The Hebrew word *shalom* is defined as "completeness, soundness, welfare, tranquility, friendship, peace." The majority of its usage refers to "fulfillment" and "completeness." The prophet and the righteous in the nation of Judah were suffering, and more suffering was to come. Their personal experience of *shalom* was in jeopardy; they were not completely alive. The suffering had diminished their quality of life.

How can we then "live" in the Hebrew sense when we are in crisis and confusion? Do we merely "grin and bear it"? Does it mean that we simply hang tough and survive our situation? I have met with many Christians who think so. They are so miserable in their suffering that they make everyone around them miserable as well. They testify that they are beating the sickness, but all the while they are barely hanging on. In the hospital, nurses and other caregivers do not like to go to their rooms. At church, people try to avoid them. Friends and relatives hesitate to call and visit. Yes, they are holding onto life, but their attitude is negative and their experience of life disenchanting. This is not what God means in "the righteous shall live…." This is not "living"! This is not experiencing *shalom*!

God is telling the prophet that the righteous will be fully alive. Their faith will restore their "vital force." Their sense or state of *sha-*

lom will be renewed. "The righteous shall live" means that they will experience wholeness and well-being. Jesus said "life more abundantly." Paul says "more than conquerors." The concept of barely making it is contrary to Scripture.

The concept of barely making it is contrary to Scripture.

The third word in Habakkuk's phrase, "the righteous shall live by his faith" is equally important to understanding this message. The Hebrew word *('emunah)* is sometimes translated *faith* and other times *faithfulness*. The two ideas cannot be separated. However, in most Old Testament usage it refers to that which faith produces—endurance, steadfastness, fidelity, integrity. If we put the two concepts together, it becomes much clearer: The righteous shall live by faith-producing steadfastness.

Here is the answer to Habakkuk's perplexity. It is not one to satisfy the philosophical mind, for the questions about God's justice in the world are not addressed. Intellectual inquiries about the character of God are not answered. God does not give reasons for his decisions. The painful, perplexing questions persist. Yet God's revelation communicates that the righteous shall be steadfast in their faithful duty to God's law. They are to continue to pray and practice their religious faith. They are to continue celebrating their faith through the rites and rituals of their church. They are to continue steadily in their devotion to God and good deeds for the Kingdom of God. They are to continue to be loyal followers of God's will. God states that this faithfulness will result in abundant living.

God is telling us that during those times of suffering and unanswered questions, we are to stay steady on the course. We are to hold firmly to the Christian values and biblical principles that have guided our decisions and direction in the past. Tragedy and other terrible trials have contributed to the spiritual shipwreck of many a good Christian sailor. The temptation is to try something else to find instant healing of the pain. There are innumerable religious groups ready to provide quick answers to the soul's distress, but these answers offer short, not sustained relief. God says, "Stay the course." The answer may be slow in coming, but it will eventually come. The people are challenged to trust Him, believing that he will do what is right and best for his own. This faith-producing steadfastness means that His people must simply "trust and obey," even without confirmation from feelings or circumstances, that God is at work.

The writer of the Hebrews included a whole chapter devoted to the wonders of faith. He recites person after person from the Old Testament who overcome great obstacles and impossible odds because of their faith. I love these concluding verses:

> Who through faith conquered kingdoms, administered justice, and gained what was promised; who shut *the mouths of lions, quenched the fury of the flames, and escaped the edge of the sword; whose weakness was turned to strength; and who became powerful in battle and routed foreign armies. Women received back their dead, raised to life again. Others were tortured and refused to be released, so that they might gain a better resurrection. Some faced jeers and flogging, while still others were chained and put in prison. They were stoned; they were sawed in two; they were put to death by the sword. They went about in sheepskins and goatskins, destitute, persecuted and mistreated—the world was not worthy of them. They wandered in deserts and mountains, and in caves and holes in the ground. These were all commended for their faith...*
> (Hebrews 11: 33–39a)

What a picture of the accomplishments of genuine faith!

They were indeed "more than conquerors." Faith in God helped these people bravely confront any and all threats to body or soul with an assurance that is uncommon. He concludes that the "world was not worthy of them." Their exercise of faith in extreme circumstances elevated them to God's sacred list of heroes.

But the question is "how." How can I rise to faith and remain steadfast in Christian living when my world is tumbling down? How can I rise to faith and remain devoted to God when my questions go unanswered and the pain persists? How can I pray and practice my faith when I don't feel like it and keep the rituals of my church when I find them meaningless? It is one thing to tell me that I should remain loyal to my faith, but how do I do it?

The painful questions can be so intense that finding the faith to be steadfast is too much for us. Well-intentioned Christians can advise us to have faith and everything will work out for us, but they don't understand that we cannot rise to faith. Our knees have been buckled by the weight of our burdens and we cannot stand. Tears flow from our eyes; we are weakened by our troubles. We want to have faith. We desire faith. But instead of faith, the questions remain and overwhelm us.

I do not like to hear Christians and ministers inconsiderately and unwisely share the contents of this verse with those who are in distress. They advise hurting people to have faith and everything will be all right. Yes, faith in God is necessary and pure faith can change circumstances. But many suffering people have lost faith. Saying "just have faith" when their whole being is crying out in anger toward God for answers is futile.

I have been called on many occasions to the hospital emergency room or to a patient's room when a patient's status changed for the worse. Though I was the hospital chaplain, often the patient's pastor and/or church leaders would be present or would visit while I was there to provide pastoral care to their people. Countless times, I listened as spiritual leaders of various Christian denominations sought to encourage the grieving. Feeling the necessity to say something to the hurting, it is just too easy to quote familiar biblical passages, say a short prayer, and quickly depart. I have watched suffering people hear the words of their spiritual leaders, confirm their acceptance of the words, and thank those who brought those words. Soon after, as I sat with these people to merely listen, they would express their truest feelings at that moment about God, religion, and the injustice and unfairness of life. Their spiritual leaders often did not hear these words. They were too busy giving the answers, so they failed to hear the questions of the soul.

I have been guilty of the same. In my early years as a minister, I found it most difficult visiting those who were experiencing deep pain. I really felt for them and wanted so desperately to say the right thing to make it better. Not only did I want to say the right thing, but it was also expected that the minister come on the scene and give the word of comfort and hope. I was playing a role—visit the troubled, give the word of God, say a prayer, and leave appropriately. Yes, those hurting need an encouraging word from a representative of God, but as I later discovered, they needed more.

I began to be honest with my own questions about the apparent injustices and unfairness of life. Watching innocent and beautiful young babies struggle to breathe and die will do that to you. Observing good, honest, and dedicated men and women of faith fight to win their personal battle with disease; talking with Christians who wanted desperately to save their marriage when one partner had dishonored the marital vows; counseling loving and committed parents who were suffering deeply because of the rebellious behavior of their child; listening to a combat surgeon confess his anguish of soul after losing another Marine on his operating table; hearing over and over the confessions of combat Marines who tell of their hidden fear or their guilt for killing; listening to mortuary affairs Marines share their horror at collecting body parts of fellow Marines after an explosion; listening to story after story of physical, emotional, and mental trauma opened my eyes slowly to see another way to provide pastoral care. Hurting people need to be heard! And they need to be heard by men and women of faith. No pronouncements of "it will be all right," "things will improve," "you can handle this," "God has a purpose in it all." No, just listening and affirming their story and their pain.

I began to listen. It was very uncomfortable at first. I battled with my own need to say or do something. Often I wondered why I was even there if I didn't rush to say what everyone expected me to say and do what everyone expected me to do. I sat with people in the surgery waiting room, I stood with people in the emergency room, I was present when the bad news was delivered. I listened as troubled people came to me for counseling. I echoed and affirmed their questions. I stopped trying to uplift them with a popular biblical text but encourage them to ask their questions and to express their pain. Depending on the situation, I may read from a psalm of lament (Psalm 13) to help them give words to their suffering.

The difference has been remarkable. When I threw away the answer book and more honestly and openly shared the pain of others, I witnessed healthy catharsis and healing. When I quit being so defensive about my faith and understood that I don't need to serve as God's lawyer, I was more free to empathize with the hurting and to provide more authentic understanding and support. I was more able to be used of God as an agent of hope and healing.

The troubled need to talk and the hurting need to be heard. If the representatives of religious faith fail to listen, then people will not get the help they need, or they will go outside the community of faith to seek it. Ministers are on the front lines of trauma intervention. Theirs is a tremendous opportunity and responsibility. If I am fully present with the person and provide appropriate intervention, then oftentimes, no other help is needed. If I fail to provide appropriate pastoral care, then professional counseling may be required. Like Habakkuk, if I can listen intently to the cries of others, then I can more authentically make intercession for them and lead them to receive the gift of faith.

*The troubled need to talk and the
hurting need to be heard.*

I suspect that Habakkuk heard the cries of the righteous in the land. He listened as the people complained about their situation and God's apparent absence. He was then able to share their burden and make intercession for the people. I am convinced that Habakkuk would have missed a great opportunity to make a difference if he had merely spoken a divine oracle from God. Because he listened and voiced the perplexity of the people, he could bring the requests to God and receive faith to face the dark days that lay ahead. Baily and Barker observe,

> Habakkuk's message is set within a backdrop of real people facing real questions about real human suffering. The prophet's questions prompted God's revelation. The revelation is centered in words that have repeatedly transformed the world; the righteous shall live by their faithfulness to God. (p. 246)

Faith will make a difference in how we recover from bad news and terrible experiences. However, there are those situations in life that throw us for a loop and we do not possess the faith to trust God. We may think that God has let us down, rejected us, or abandoned us. I have talked with pastors who have been misunderstood and maligned by Christians and churches, and their faith in God hangs by a thread. I have counseled Christians who confess to being used and abused as long as they can remember; betrayed by significant others in their life, they find it almost impossible to trust anyone—including God. I have counseled mature Christians who silently suffered for a long time with the thought that God had taken a leave of absence from them. Telling them to trust God and to believe that this is for their good is not "healing the brokenhearted." I must hear their story, stand by them, and support them as they struggle to open their souls to the birth of faith.

For many years, as I preached from Habakkuk, "the just shall live by faith" was the crowning concept of this book. I announced that this is the answer to the soul suffering from unanswered questions. Any suffering can be endured if one has this faith-producing steadfastness. It was easy to find illustrations and stories of saintly souls who turned suffering and troubles into positive testimonies of glory to God. I stand in awe of those who have overcome some very serious obstacles and witness to the faithfulness of God to his people. I am still convinced that faith in God can change how we look at our troubles and how we respond to our troubles. Faith-producing steadfastness can get all of us through the dark nights of the soul when unanswered questions attack our peace; if, and for emphasis I repeat *if,* we are gifted with the faith-producing steadfastness to which Habakkuk alludes.

But I am still left with troubled people who don't have this faith. My chaplain colleague, whose wife of ten years started an affair that led to a divorce, could not for an extended period of time, no matter how hard he tried, find the faith he so urgently needed to trust God. I know and have provided pastoral care to many others who are not yet there where God is seen as faithful and the situations in life are viewed positively. They question God's faithfulness; they cannot help it. They cannot see any good in what has happened or in what is happening to them. They are unable to muster faith to trust in God or to remain steadfast in their Christian beliefs.

While on a student missionary journey to Guyana, South America, my wife Donna and I were in an area without electricity. I shall never forget returning to our sleeping quarters each evening after service. The moonless night was as dark as I have ever witnessed. Until a lantern was lit, I was afraid to take even one step in the darkness. I heard the sounds of abundant wildlife and insects, and I felt totally vulnerable to the environment. When the guide approached and lit the lantern, confidence replaced the cautiousness. I was then ready to go forward.

The darkness that permeates the lives of some people is so heavy that they are too afraid to move. You can tell them over and over again "to have faith," but their present reality is the blackness of night. It is not until there is light, though small and flickering, that they will proceed with courage and confidence. The presence of God brings the light.

In my thinking, then, there has to be more than God's telling Habakkuk that "the just shall live by faith." This announcement, though life-changing for some, doesn't really help those who are struggling with serious questions of faith. This is no different than the "just have faith" theology of some today. Surely, Habakkuk knew he should have faith in God. He knew to continue practicing his faith because he is engaging in prayer to God. But his is a *crisis of faith*. And telling those who are experiencing serious doubts about God and religion to simply believe is too much to ask. Yet at the same time, there may not be any answers to their questions. So what do they do? What do we do? What do I do when I do not have the faith-producing steadfastness to which God calls us and I am overwhelmed with my burden?

We wait on God. Even when we cannot believe, we simply and prayerfully wait. But like Habakkuk, we wait with personal and sometimes prolonged visits to our "watchtower." As we shall see in the next chapter, Habakkuk's waiting results in more than a revelation "the just shall live by faith." He needs more than God telling him to have faith, and at times, so do we. His waiting is met by a visitor with a light.

The Presumptuous Will Perish

The vision received by Habakkuk—the message he is to billboard for all to read—clearly contrasts the righteous and the wicked. As we have considered, "the righteous shall live by faith-producing steadfastness." The wicked, however, live by their devices. God states that they are "puffed up," colloquially "swollen-headed" and "proud." They are characterized by their pride and arrogance. Though a particular group of people (Babylonians) may be in mind, the message is for all. The puffed up will eventually burst! They will ultimately fail. It happened to the greedy and brutal Babylonians. They became so "puffed up" with their power, pride, and perverseness that they died. The Persians conquered Babylon in 538 BC.

God is informing his prophet that while the righteous remain loyal to the law and steadfast to their faith in spite of their unanswered questions, the wicked may temporarily have the upper hand, but they will ultimately fail. The righteous that stay on course, notwithstanding their confusion and conflict, shall live; the wicked that play god shall die. The outcomes have been determined. Faithfulness to God reaps its rewards; pride, however, comes before a fall, and tyranny has within it the seeds of its own demise and destruction.

Habakkuk is instructed to place this message on the bulletin board for all to read. Even the runner who passes by quickly should be able to get a glimpse of the words to ponder as he continues. In modern vernacular, the message should be placed so clearly and creatively that all web surfers will hit it. God doesn't want anyone to miss this revelation. The righteous, by remaining steadfast, shall live; but the proud, who are puffed up with a sense of their own importance and who possess a perverse character and practice a blatant disregard for the welfare of others, shall perish.

It has become clear to Habakkuk that the Babylonians, though used of God to discipline His people, will suffer an even greater destruction. Any nation or kingdom or individual who lives by his own law in willful defiance of the law of God shall not continue. History verifies the veracity of this message.

Any nation or kingdom or individual
who lives by his own law
in willful defiance of the law of God
shall not continue.

Five "Woe" Oracles

The remainder of chapter 2 (vv. 6–20) amplifies this revelation given to Habakkuk that the presumptuous will perish. A clear message is directed against the Babylonians and all who emulate their wickedness. Five "woe" oracles are announced upon them; their fate has been sealed, and this first woe and funeral song tell why:

> Will not all these take up a proverb against him,
> And a taunting riddle against him, and say,

Woe to him who increases
What is not his—how long?
And to him who loads himself with many pledges?
Will not your creditors rise up suddenly?
Will they not awaken who oppress you?
And you will become their booty.
Because you have plundered many nations,
All the remnant of the people shall plunder you,
Because of men's blood
And the violence of the land and the city,
And of all who dwell in it. (Habakkuk 2:6–8)

The *first "woe"* of impending doom identifies a common practice of conquering nations. They used their power to become prosperous at the expense of the plundered. Their insatiable greed led to stealing and violence. "How long?" the oppressed people of God ask will the proud plunder the poor? The answer is implicit in the riddle. Not for long! The Babylonians shall themselves tremble for they will be plundered by the nations and peoples it has plundered. They shall reap what they have sown.

Power can be used for good or evil. Power can be used to heal or to hurt. Power can be used to give or to take. Power can be used to empower or to dominate others. The wicked described in this initial "woe" have employed their power to satisfy their own lust for more. Their abuse of power rapes and robs the resources of others; their abuse of power oppresses and overwhelms the powerless; their abuse of power violates the human rights of others. Their misuse of power will be accountable to them.

Through the prophet Habakkuk, God is letting his beleaguered people know that their oppressors shall suffer their own destruction because of their arrogant behavior and misuse of power. They are being reminded that they are to remain steady in their faithfulness, despite the abuse they endure by unethical, powerful people. They cry out to God, "How long must we endure this tragedy at the hands of these invaders?"

God says, "Soon, I will wreak havoc upon the oppressors."

There is instruction here for all who would listen. Possessing power is an awesome responsibility. To use power to empower others is biblical; to misuse power is a great evil. In this first declaration of judgment, it is clear that the "puffed up" who abuse their power will be punished. Their wrongful use of power will eventually lead to their fall.

Even a cursory reading of the daily news will reveal another powerful person's arrest for unethical and illegal behavior. The hunger for power is for some an insatiable appetite. They will cheat, steal, lie, oppress, abuse, harass, and engage in evil activities to gain power and to keep power. It is a temptation for many leaders. God is showing Habakkuk their final outcome: "Hold steady. Keep the faith. God's people will win in the end." But does this really help now? How can we hang on and hold on?"

But does this revelation actually help the prophet and the people in their present situation? It may be good to know that evil ones will one day reap their just rewards, but what about the pain and suffering I am going through today? For Habakkuk and the people of Judah, the eventual demise and destruction of Babylon does not change their current reality. The Babylonians are still coming. They will destroy the land and the holy city, Jerusalem, and the holy temple. The people of Judah will be destitute and thousands will be hauled off to Babylon and forced to live there against their will.

Okay, God, I understand that the day will come when those who are so puffed up with power that they abuse and oppress others will themselves be punished, but what about now? Why allow them to come at all? Why not stop their advance and military victory? Isn't there another way for us to learn the lessons that we need to learn without the total devastation of our homes and livelihood? This is just too much to take. The revelation is clear, but the questions still remain? "Keep on keeping on" is easy to say until you lose everything. Remaining steady in faithfulness is good spiritual guidance, but how do I do it when my world is crashing down? "How long?" the people pray.

This *second "woe"* indicts lofty ambition divorced from noble character and ethical principles.

> Woe to him who covets evil gain for his house,
> That he may set his nest on high,
> That he may be delivered from the power of
> disaster!
>
> You give shameful counsel to your house,
> Cutting off many peoples,
> And sin against your soul.
> For the stone will cry out from the wall,
> And the beam from the timbers will answer it.
> (Habakkuk 2:9–11)

The Babylonians coveted the status of most supreme power and they built this status on the substance and suffering of others. Their ambition was to be the greatest; the means to get there did not matter to them. In so doing, they brought shame to their own house. Even the stones and wood of their houses, plundered from others, are witnesses of their unethical behavior.

Ambition is noble; ambition apart from ethical conduct is ignoble. Many a nation and person has succumbed to the temptation of sacrificing all to reach the pinnacle of success. They desire to set their "nest on high," secure and safe, and they shamefully engage in unjust practices to accomplish it. To aspire to higher office or a climb in the professional ladder is commendable, for God calls his people to do their very best, but to deny one's identity as Christian in the process leads to disgrace and dishonor.

Within any organization, there are those who want the "nest on high" so passionately that it becomes their top priority. It becomes acceptable to use any means to gain their goal. Befriending the right people, securing the right jobs, and receiving the right evaluations and rewards by any and all means can easily become the "sin against your soul." Compromise of ethical principles is a constant threat to those seeking the "nest on high."

God's revelation makes it clear that any success which comes through evil gain will bring shame to one's house! "The house of the wicked will be overthrown; but the tent of the upright shall flourish" (Proverbs 14:11).

The revelation received by the prophet Habakkuk continues to show him that those who employ evil means to attain and keep their "nest on high" will themselves experience the "woe" of God. But meanwhile, the prophet is looking to what is coming directly at him and his people in real time: total destruction. So how does this help him in his current crisis? There must be more!

The *third "woe"* continues the teaching of the first two.

> Woe to him who builds a town with bloodshed,
> Who establishes a city by iniquity!
> Behold, is it not of the Lord of hosts
> That the peoples labor to feed the fire,
> And nations weary themselves in vain?
> For the earth will be filled
> With the knowledge of the glory of the Lord,
> As the waters cover the sea. (Habakkuk 2:12–14)

Pride that abuses power and makes ambition supreme will result in a great fall. In this taunt, it is even clearer that the nation, kingdom, or people who expand their interests with bloodshed and crime will collapse. All of their evil activities only "feed the fire" and "weary themselves in vain." It will all come to nothing. "Unless the Lord builds the house, they labor in vain who build it" (Psalm 127:1).

Pride which abuses power and makes ambition
supreme will result in a great fall.

The perplexing question that Habakkuk asked in the beginning about the violence and wickedness in the land and whether God is going to do anything about it has been answered. As the righteous live by remaining steadfast and on course, the proud will be punished. In each "woe," the judgment of God is announced upon those who live by their own rules without regard for the commandments of God. However, at the end of this third "woe," God makes known that his ultimate purpose is not merely to punish the proud, but to fill the earth "with the knowledge of the glory of the Lord."

The proud, perverse, and powerful Babylonians may rule for a season. Others who build their towns and cities by violence and crime may follow. Yes, we may witness the success of people who abuse their power, harass subordinates, hinder workers from progress, and who covet the rewards and accolades for themselves alone. Sometimes, we may even look with envy upon their success, but their time will come. God's purposes and people will prevail. God will be known in the earth, and His presence will fill the earth as waters cover the sea. Again, "stay steady, remain faithful" through all that life brings you and look for the rainbow of God's promise.

In this *fourth "woe,"* the suppression and violation of human rights is indicted.

> Woe to him who gives drink to his neighbor,
> Pressing him to your bottle,
> Even to make him drink,
> That you may look on his nakedness!
> You are filled with shame instead of glory.
> You also—drink!
> And be exposed as uncircumcised!
> The cup of the Lord's right hand will be turned
>   against you,
> And utter shame will be on your glory.
> For the violence done to Lebanon will cover you,
> And the plunder of beasts which made them
>   afraid,
> Because of men's blood
> And the violence of the land and the city,

And of all who dwell in it. (Habakkuk 2:15–17)

The Babylonian lust of hedonistic celebrations is employed as a metaphor for the prophet's purposes. The Babylonians were notorious for their wild parties celebrating their successes. The heavy drinking led to an array of evil behavior. The captured peoples were enticed and enlisted to join in these parties, and their drunkenness and nakedness became a spectacle for the Babylonians. The vanquished were publicly shamed in the guise of pleasurable celebration. The Babylonians delighted in the total humiliation of their subjects. So God states that they shall experience the same shame that they inflicted upon others.

Though drunkenness is highlighted, the real issue is the deceitfulness which befriends people with indications of good intentions only to turn against them. The Babylonians violated the basic human right of all those created in the image of God—human dignity. They and all other nations and people will be held accountable to God's justice regarding how we treat our fellowman—friend or foe.

This "woe" also indicts the Babylonians for raping the forests of Lebanon of trees and wildlife. Lebanon was noted for its thick forests with its stately cedars and abundant animal life. The Babylonians ravaged these forests for their own benefit. God holds human beings accountable for their treatment of His earth and its resources. Whether we like environmental regulations or not, God has entrusted the earth to our care. We are the earth's caretakers; environmental concerns are a spiritual responsibility. The Babylonians and all other people will be accountable to God for how we have cared for his creation.

In this *fifth* and *final* "*woe*," the idolatrous worship practiced by the Babylonians is exposed as folly.

> What profit is the image, that its maker should
>   carve it,
> The molded image, a teacher of lies,
> That the maker of its mold should trust in it,

To make mute idols?
Woe to him who says to wood,
"Awake!"
To silent stone, "Arise! It shall teach!"
Behold, it is overlaid with gold and silver,
Yet in it there is no breath at all.
But the Lord is in His holy temple.
Let all the earth keep silence before Him.
    (Habakkuk 2:18–20)

The designing and making of wooden and molten idols for the purpose of worship is totally irrational. These products of human hands are without breath and without the capacity to give any assistance.

The Babylonians put their trust in gods made by the skill of craftsmen from material of the earth. These idols are deaf and dumb. They cannot hear the prayers of the people. These idols lack any ability to give direction, help, or comfort for they are lifeless. They are "nothings" and it is unreasonable and foolish to rely upon them.

In sharp contrast to the lifeless idols made by human invention is the God of Israel who is in his holy temple. Habakkuk's God is not a creation of human hands; He is the great Creator. The temple in Jerusalem becomes a metaphor for the universe, which is filled with the presence of God. Habakkuk's God is so great and awesome that all the earth is called to silence before him.

It is only fitting that chapter 2 ends with this sublime tribute to God. Habakkuk presented to God his deepest concerns about the way things are in the land and his confusion as to why God appears to be doing nothing about it. After hearing and writing the revelation of God for all to read, he is now convinced that the Lord has not forgotten them or forsaken them. His presence fills the earth; unlike the man-made gods of Babylon, his God hears him when he prays.

Though Habakkuk now understands more fully that God will act according to his own schedule to punish the proud and perverse, still all of his questions have not been answered. He knows, however, that to live a full and enriched life, he must have faith-producing steadfastness. He must stay on course. God's answer that "the righteous shall live by faith" shows him that he must continue to trust God's process and believe that in the end it will all be settled as good to his life's account. But the how has not been answered. How can I rise to faith when my spiritual legs fail me? How can I "live by faith" when I am sinking in the storms that rage within and around me? Yes, I believe that God will eventually balance it all out and the righteous will win, but what about now? What about the grief that totally disrupts my quality of life now? What about this disease that is destroying my body and ravaging my mind of all positive thoughts? Now, I know that the evil ones will not win, but it looks like they are winning now. So I want to have faith. I really want to believe and practice my faith. I truly wish church and spiritual rituals meant something to me today, but my devastating questions have vanquished my spirit and traumatized my soul. I can find no meaning in my religion right now. God, I need more that an exhortation to remain steady and believe that good will prevail. The Babylonians may face their own demise and downfall by the Persians, but the prophet and the people must first face the full onslaught of Babylonian power and might. Their armies are just over the horizon. Judah is in their sights. They will demolish the country, and take all the sacred and costly items from the temple in Jerusalem, and then burn it and force nearly five thousand people into exile in faraway Babylon. The prophet Jeremiah in chapter 52 verses 4b–30 gives a picture of the destruction:

> Nebuchadnezzar king of Babylon marched against Jerusalem with his whole army. They camped outside the city and built siege works all around it.... By the ninth day of the fourth month famine in the city had become so severe that there was not food for the people to eat. Then the city wall was broken through, and the whole army fled.... He set fire to the temple of the Lord, the royal palace and

all the houses of Jerusalem. Every important build-
ing was burned down. The whole Babylonian army
under the commander of the imperial guard broke
down all the walls around Jerusalem. Nebuzaradan
the command of the guard carried into exile some of
the poorest people and those who remain in the city,
along with the rest of the craftsmen.... So Judah
went into captivity, away from her land... There
were 4,600 people in all.

God had forewarned Habakkuk of the coming catastrophe. He knew what to expect, but he vehemently had questioned how God could really do it to His chosen people. He was told to live by faith and to keep steady in the faith even without adequate and satisfying answers to his personal questions. He knows what to do, but now he will learn how to do it. Habakkuk has received a word from God about living by faith and about the ultimate destruction of their enemies, but he is about to encounter the glory of God that will give to him the gift of faith to stay on course.

CHAPTER 3

The Praise of the Prophet

Commitment to Celebration

Chapter 3 contains the climax of Habakkuk's experience and the crowning jewel of his book. This final chapter and its concluding psalm complete the book.

This ode is the crescendo of a musical piece written for worship in the temple. Its opening and closing statements indicate that it may have been employed as an independent psalm for worship apart from the book. Its inclusion here, however, is no accident. This chapter brings to a grand and glorious conclusion the concerns and complaints of a faithful and sincere prophet of God. Without it, we have God's word for the righteous to remain steadfast, but no revelation on how we are to possess such faith. The book is incomplete without chapter 3; our personal search for answers is incomplete without the message it contains.

The third chapter begins with a title verse: "A prayer of Habakkuk the prophet, on Shinionoth." The presence of this verse suggests that this section of the book existed independently of the other two chapters. The meaning of "on Shinionoth" is unclear. Scholars agree, however, that the term is likely a musical notation for the singers and/or musicians indicating the melody, tune, accompaniment, or some other musical instruction. The use of *Selah* in verse

3 is used only here outside the Psalms and appears to be another musical instruction. The final statement, "To the Chief Musician. With my stringed instruments," adds further evidence that this psalm was sung in Temple worship as an act of praise to God. It is a psalm of thanksgiving to be sung in joyous harmony by those who, like Habakkuk, have made the successful journey from complaint to celebration. It is Habakkuk's final tribute to the God who is his strength.

Prayer for God's Intervention

Following the title verse identifying the writing as a prayer of Habakkuk, there is the only petition in the entire chapter. Verse 2 contains the prayer of the prophet:

> O Lord, I have heard Your speech and was afraid;
> O Lord, revive Your work in the midst of the
> years!
> In the midst of the years make it known;
> In wrath remember mercy.

The prophet trembles in the presence of God. The mighty deeds of God displayed throughout her sacred history to save and discipline Israel produce within Habakkuk a genuine sense of holy fear or "awe." He has heard the report of what God is planning to do. His people will be disciplined once again; he understands it is now inevitable. But Habakkuk is not finished with his intercession. He prays for the merciful intervention of God.

The "holy fear" or "awe" that the prophet felt is not unique to this man of God. Moses stood in the presence of God and was commanded to take off his sandals because the ground was holy. Isaiah envisioned God upon a throne surrounded by an angelic choir singing "holy, holy, holy, Lord God Almighty," and he fell to his face. Habakkuk stated at the end of chapter 2 that the Lord is in his temple and all the earth should be in silence before Him. But where is this "silence before Him?" Where is this "holy fear" and "awe" of the Lord God?

During my student missionary trip to India, I visited Hindu temples and holy sites. I watched and studied those who engaged in prayer to the numerous Hindu gods. I was impressed with the spirit of reverence and sense of "awe" that the worshippers possessed as they entered the places of worship and offered their prayers. Some would kneel, but many would fall upon their faces in reverence to their god (s). I saw the same in South Korea, Thailand, and Japan at Buddhist temples. Speaking was not allowed. There was total silence before their god(s).

In my military travels, I try to visit many places of worship to better understand the religion of the people. I especially enjoy visiting the cathedrals. People enter throughout the day and evening to light a candle and pray. The respect for the "house of God" and the reverence for God is tangible. Silence is required.

Our modern church services are often more full of fellowship and singing. These are valuable aspects of worship which I appreciate, but sometimes I wonder if we have forgotten the God who makes prophets tremble. Perhaps we should arrive in the early quiet moments to focus on the sacred hour before us. Perhaps more stillness and silence is needed to calm our hurried minds and bodies. Hushed moments can bring the most meaningful awareness of God's presence.

Habakkuk intercedes once again for his people. Judgment is inevitable; distress and destruction are coming upon the people of God. Habakkuk does not pray that it will not come. He prays that God will renew His work. The work of God which began with the call of this people to be His own and their decision to follow Him needs repair. The people of God need new life. They need revival. The prophet pleads that in the execution of God's wrath, by way of the Babylonians, He will not forget mercy. Habakkuk knows his people have erred in their ways and he has come to understand that they will be punished, but he moves beyond this to a greater vision.

He hopes that God will remember to show mercy to His people and renew their spiritual devotion.

This prayer of the prophet is also his personal petition for spiritual renewal. Yes, he is greatly concerned for the well-being of his people. He wants them to learn the lessons that God wants to teach them. However, Habakkuk himself needs revival. He has struggled with deeply personal perplexity about the ways of God. His questions concerning the justice and compassion of God have taken their toll on his spiritual life. He needs for God to renew His work in the "midst of the years" of his own life. He has suffered doubt and distress. He has harbored anger toward God. Habakkuk needs God to renew him.

The search for answers drains us emotionally, mentally, and spiritually. Our questions of God and confusion about the ways of God produce spiritual dehydration. We need the refreshing waters of God's spirit to renew our faith and to give to us the spiritual strength to be steadfast in our devotion and duty. Habakkuk's prayer can become our prayer as we plead for God to revive His work in us.

God's Visit to Habakkuk

God answered the prayer of the prophet. Habakkuk has a mysterious encounter with God. He describes his experience in beautiful Hebrew poetry. The language of the Psalms is employed to communicate the indescribable—an appearance of God in power and glory (theophany). God's spiritual visitation to Habakkuk renews his faith. It is the culmination of his spiritual journey from complaint to celebration.

> God came from Teman,
> The Holy One from Mount Paran. Selah.
> His glory covered the heavens,
> And the earth was full of His praise.
> His brightness was like the light;
> He had rays flashing from His hand,

And there His power was hidden.
Before Him went pestilence,
And fever followed at His feet,
He stood and measured the earth;
He looked and startled the nations,
And the everlasting mountains
were scattered,
The perpetual hills bowed,
His ways are everlasting.
I saw the tents of Cushan in affliction;
The curtains of the land of Midian trembled.
O Lord, were You displeased with the rivers,
Was Your anger against the rivers,
Was Your wrath against the sea,
That You rode on Your horses,
Your chariots of salvation?
Your bow was made quite ready;
Oaths were sworn over Your arrows. Selah.
You divided the earth with rivers.
The mountains saw You and trembled;
The overflowing of the water passed by.
The deep uttered its voice,
And lifted its hands on high.
The sun and moon stood still in their habitation;
At the light of Your arrows they went,
At the shining of Your glittering spear.
You marched through the land in indignation;
You trampled the nations in anger.
You went forth for the salvation of Your people,
For salvation with Your Anointed.
You struck the head from the house of the wicked,
By laying bare from foundation to neck. Selah
You thrust through with his own arrows
The head of his villages.
They came out like a whirlwind to scatter me;

> Their rejoicing was like feasting on the poor in
> secret.
> You walked through the sea with Your horses,
> Through the heap of great waters.
> When I heard, my body trembled;
> My lips quivered at the voice;
> Rottenness entered my bones;
> And I trembled in myself,
> That I might rest in the day of trouble.
> When he comes up to the people,
> He will invade them with his troops. (Habakkuk
> 3:3–16)

Habakkuk uses the imagery most familiar to the worshipping community in describing the manifestation of God. Two of Israel's pivotal events in the formation of her religious faith, the exodus from Egypt and the giving of the Law at Mt. Sinai, serve as the backdrop for this appearance of God to the prophet. We do not need to labor over the form or content of this poem to fully appreciate that Habakkuk had a mysterious and mystical experience of the Holy One, which thoroughly transforms his outlook on life. The God who came in the past and performed His mighty acts on behalf of His people has come to the praying prophet who needed his faith in God renewed.

Since words are inadequate to describe an appearance of God, poetic expressions and imagery taken from his culture and religion are employed to make the meaning clear. The poetic devices used by writers of psalms are not to be taken literally; they are word pictures which aid in understanding what is most incomprehensible—the nature of God. Habakkuk is so overwhelmed by the brilliant light of God's presence and the awesome might of God's power that he intuitively knows that everything will work out all right. It has in the past as God displayed His power to deliver the people of Israel from Egypt's bondage and to escort them to the Promised Land.

Habakkuk now knows that God will again work His mighty deeds "for the salvation" of His people.

Habakkuk's personal experience of the presence of God is critical to understanding his recovery from the pit of anger and doubt to spiritual renewal. The visitation of God described in Hebrew poetry was personal and transformative. It marked the beginning of his transition to spiritual recovery.

God's visit to a person of faith, who is struggling to stay afloat spiritually, can take many and varied forms. No one can prescribe how God will visit. It could be through a sermon, a song, or the words of a trusted friend or counselor; through meditation, Scripture, or nature. I have experienced the divine in and through all of these means. It happens when we perceive that God is present and that He is speaking to us personally. In our spiritual dilemma and unrest, God breaks through with His grace. He changes our perspective about our problems. The encounter changes our response to our questions and confusion. His visit leads us to renewal of soul and spirit. We are strengthened, we are empowered, we are now enabled to move forward once again in our spiritual journey.

I can recall several times in Iraq when the presence of God inspired me to faith. I had heard that we had multiple wounded inbound to Fallujah Surgical. Immediately, I walked to the medical area. I visited several who needed evacuation to a higher level of intervention. I then went outside to speak to their fellow Marines who had brought them from the battlefield. I knew they had been terribly impacted. After I spoke to them I was shocked to see their reaction. They found a football, took off their combat gear, and proceeded to play a game in the pouring rain and mud. They played tackle football to deal with their anguish. They let it all out on the field of play. They were covered in mud, and I didn't know when they would be able to get a shower, but they were dealing with their grief and pain. I stood, watched, and felt like I was in the presence of God and standing on holy ground. These young eighteen- and nineteen-year-old Marines were letting go of their fear and anger, if but for a short time, before heading back to combat. I simply said "Thank you, God" for their opportunity to find a moment of peace in the midst of such turmoil. I cannot watch a football game today without remembering this scene.

On another occasion, I was feeling very tired and angry at the number of wounded we had been seeing. I was called again to Fallujah Surgical to see injured Marines. I visited a room with a young Marine who had a very serious leg wound. I spoke to him and offered a prayer. After my prayer, he looked up to me through his physical pain and asked in a whisper if I could get *his* chaplain. I was the senior chaplain for all chaplains in Western Iraq, but that did not matter to him. He desperately wanted *his* unit chaplain. Almost immediately, he walked in. I shall never forget the look on this Marine's face as he saw *his* chaplain coming near him. I stepped back and stood amazed at the relationship this young chaplain had with his Marines. I shed tears at what I witnessed, and I knew God was present in that encounter. My heart was uplifted.

On yet another occasion, we had multiple Marines wounded and burned. They were mostly females who worked at guard posts to pat down local women wanting to come into the city. A civilian truck had deliberately crashed into the side of one of our trucks hitting the gas tank. The truck caught fire and several of the women were burned. As they arrived, I saw that one of my chaplains was providing ministry to them as he was able. I did not interfere but rather stepped aside and prayed for the Marines and their chaplain. He would occasionally come to me to update me on the status of different ones. Fellow Marines gathered and waited. Anguish of spirit was evident upon every face. I felt their pain. I was angry at war and the suffering that it causes. But in those moments I felt the presence of God as people silently prayed, doctors provided intervention, and as the chaplain ministered to the wounded.

We must be careful not to limit God by our expectations of how He should visit us. When we may not expect it, God visits us with grace, strength, and peace even though the storm may still be raging. As we practice the presence of God, we can be aware of His coming and open to His healing mercy and abundant strength in the worse of circumstances. Written by my wife Donna Milliner, the following poem amplifies this thought.

Assurance

As midnight settles 'round you—
A future glad seems gone;
Fear not the darkened hour
The darkest precedes dawn.
As surely as the ocean tides,
A new day's going to break;
And with the rising sun of hope,
The next step you will take.
With God's hand holding onto yours,
His voice of comfort hear,
Lean on His everlasting arms,
For He is very near.
Walk forth into the morning bright,
Expect discovery,
For through the unknown way ahead
He's made a path for thee.
You've promises to be fulfilled,
So claim the peace you seek;
God's faithful in His strength which is
Perfected when you're weak.(*NightSongs*, p. 3)

Habakkuk's Ode of Celebration

The third chapter and the revelation of Habakkuk end with an ode celebrating the triumph of faith. The joyous outcome to Habakkuk's painful journey is remarkable. It stands in sharp contrast to the prophet's pain in chapter 1. People seriously wonder how someone can question God so vehemently and later proclaim unwavering faith in God. I am convinced it is because of his divine visitation. Charles Taylor in *The Book of Habakkuk, The Interpreter's Bible,* observes:

> *Strange as it may appear, the psalm literature—outside the canonical Psalter—reaches one of the topmost peaks in these five lines. The author's religion does not defer its dividends. In the very midst of his destitution he finds reason to exult and rejoice; living by his faithfulness, he finds life's supreme good that lifts him to high places above material calamities. (p. 1002)*

This psalm is the creation of a person who has been renewed spiritually. Habakkuk had heard the word of God. He knew that the righteous were to remain steady, on course, and they would experience the "*shalom*" of God. But it was the divine light that penetrated the soul of this man of God that transformed his outlook on life. Gailey and Kelly in *The Layman's Bible Commentary: Micah, Nahum, Habakkuk, Zephaniah, Haggai, Zechariah, Malachi* note that "[T]he real and vital presence of God gives him strength and a sense of triumph which goes beyond the patience and perseverance called for by the declaration, 'The righteous shall live by his faith'" (p. 69). A visit from God always changes our outlook.

A visit from God always changes our outlook.

These five lines of Hebrew poetry are unparalleled in their pronouncement of soulful celebration whatever the hardships of life. Here Old Testament religion reaches its peak—faith that triumphs in the midst of inexplicable suffering is the gift of the "Sovereign Lord."

> Though the fig tree does not bud
> and there are no grapes on the vines,
> though the olive crop fails
> and the fields produce no food,
> though there are no sheep in the pen

and no cattle in the stalls,
yet, I will rejoice in the Lord,
I will be joyful in God my Savior.
The Sovereign Lord is my strength;
he makes my feet like the feet of a deer,
he enables me to go on the heights.
(Habakkuk 3:3:17–19)

This psalm of Habakkuk stands in unequaled splendor among the songs of Israel. Under the influence of the Spirit of God, the prophet breaks forth into rapturous rejoicing. The inspired testimony of the prophet of God is contagious in its bold declaration and joyous spirit. He states without hesitation in the strongest of language that he "will rejoice in the Lord" whatever circumstances may exist.

The Magnitude of the Suffering

My first chaplain's call in Camp Fallujah was to a group of Marines who had just experienced a tragedy. While cleaning his rifle, a Marine discharged his weapon and killed the Marine next to him. A group of Marines were in the room and witnessed the event. The shock was upon every face. The questions were obvious as I entered and spoke to them. "Why, God?" "Is this an omen of things to come?" These were kids who were in high school the previous year and now they see the death of one of their buddies. Shock. Confusion. Anger. Fear. Grief. Trauma. And these were only the first weeks of their twelve-month war-zone deployment. More tragedy and trauma were ahead of them.

People attempt to make sense out of such tragedies. They seek a faith to understand and to accept things that cannot be changed. Psychiatrist Kenneth Pargament notes that, "[I]n crisis and catastrophe, spirituality is often intertwined in the struggle to comprehend the seemingly incomprehensible and to manage the seemingly unmanageable" (p. 3). Christians read the Bible and pray. Many talk to a pastor or counselor. They desperately want to comprehend and to manage. Habakkuk did the same. But now, after the divine and mysterious visit, he cites all the troubles that may come to him and the people of Judah, from a new perspective.

My chaplain's assistant and I stood at the helicopter pad on a dark night waiting for transport to visit one of our camps. We watched as mortar rounds were being shot off in the distance toward our camp. We were totally exposed, but the rounds were landing elsewhere in our compound. Often the sirens would blare indicating incoming rounds. After a while, one gets used to the alarm. On one particular occasion, my deputy and I were in the chow hall when the sirens were heard across the camp. We were watching Shania Twain in concert on the television set and eating ice cream—a welcomed escape from our reality. We briefly looked at one another as Marines scrambled to get to the safe, concrete barriers. We knew that the safe barrier was too far away to get to before the rockets stopped, so we smiled at each other as we took our chances, and continued to watch TV and enjoy our dessert. The people of Judah would soon hear the sound of the enemy at their gates, and there would be no bunker of safety into which they could run for shelter.

What Habakkuk describes is the worst of possibilities. Habakkuk envisions complete destitution. His words describe the loss of every-thing. Habakkuk is convinced that judgment is coming to Judah. That judgment may mean the total devastation of the economy of the land: The destruction of the fig trees, the emptiness of the vines, the failure of the olive and fields to produce, and the slaughter of the sheep and the cattle represent the worst scenario. These descriptive phrases depict the most catastrophic circumstances that could come upon the land.

The six conditional clauses introduced by "though" ascend from least importance to greatest impact. The suffering then ranges from a minor problem or inconvenience ("fig tree does not bud") to a major catastrophe ("no sheep in the pen and no cattle in the stalls"). Whether the prophet refers to each occurrence as a separate and isolated problem or the whole as a total loss of livelihood and provisions, he indicates that his response will be the same. "Though" he encounters one or all of these circumstances, "yet" he will rejoice in the Lord.

There is no scale to rate suffering. It is personal. Each person's experience of life is unique. We all evaluate our circumstances differently. Habakkuk's description of suffering covers the complete range of all we can imagine. He wants us to know that wherever we may be along the spectrum of suffering, God can give a song. Habakkuk pledged to rejoice whatever the suffering.

We cannot know what another person is feeling. We do not know the level of the hurt or pain experienced by a friend or family member. Far too often, assumptions are made and expressed about another person's problems based upon our own evaluation of the event. We cannot know the hidden issues and suppressed pain that even an apparent minor problem can surface. It is imperative then that we make no assumptions about how a person should or should not respond to a crisis. There should be no judgment; the sufferer alone knows the intensity of the hurt and the severity of their crisis. God makes no judgments for the Scripture states, "Cast all your anxiety on Him, because He cares for you" (1 Peter 5:7). *All* includes the minor, annoying inconveniences of everyday existence to the sudden, unexpected tragedies of life. Peter says to give it all to Jesus. Hold nothing back. Take every burden to God in prayer.

The human response to suffering is as diverse and unique as each individual. We begin learning from an early age ways to react to bad news and ways to respond to personal or family suffering. As we mature, we make adjustments to our personal system of emotional responses. Most frequently, our prescribed mode of response to life's ebb and flow suits us well, but there are those occasions and periods when all our learned and practiced responses are tested to the maximum and we must develop new response mechanisms to cope.

By all outward appearances and among my peers and colleagues, I was functioning extremely well. They did not know the raging storm within my mind and spirit. We cannot always know what dark and dangerous thoughts another person may be experiencing. Their pain and heartache may not be visible to others to see.

Within our first month in Fallujah, the Navy Seabees built a wooden hut to serve as our office spaces. It was in an enclosed, walled area. When the artillery fired the sound was loud and the sound waves reverberated off the walls. But at month seven, something changed. I will forever remember the day and feeling. I was walking outside when the big guns started firing. Same sound. Loud. The ground shook. But this day was different. I didn't just hear the noise, I felt the noise. It penetrated to the nerves of my body. The sound hurt. And it was this way after each outgoing fire until I left. No one knew what I felt.

I wonder if anyone but God knew of Habakkuk's intense agony of soul. Perhaps, the prophet expressed only to God in his private prayers what he was feeling. What we do know is that He personally and mysteriously encountered God and his outlook changed drastically.

Habakkuk demonstrates a God-given response for all seasons and situations of life. Whatever the magnitude of the suffering, Habakkuk has been empowered with the strength of God to "rejoice in the Lord." No, he may never understand the reason for his personal crisis; no, his questions may never be answered; no, his suffering and his circumstances may not change; however, God has blessed him with a renewed outlook and a revived spiritual strength. He is divinely "enabled" to sing a song of rejoicing.

In their hit song "Even If," the Christian band *Mercy Me* highlights this truth. The song opens with a confession that "losing bad" is a present problem and "right now I just can't" tell people that it will be all right. "A little faith is all I have, right now," and even if God does not "save through the fire," "my hope is in You alone."

God is acknowledged as able to change the circumstances. But note the ending, "even if you don't, my hope is in you alone." "Why—because "it is well with my soul."

The Magnanimity of His Strength

The response of the prophet is atypical. Instead of lamentation, there is rejoicing. Habakkuk proclaims, "Yet I will rejoice in the Lord." In spite of all the suffering which will come to his people and the land of his fathers, the prophet exults in his renewed faith. Habakkuk has been strengthened and enabled by the Lord to stay on course, to remain faithful, whatever the situation. He then utters this majestic affirmation of faith.

Here is the real answer to "just have faith." What Habakkuk was unable to do, the Lord enabled him to do. The answers to the *whys* may not have come, but strength to sustain him through his suffering has come to him. The questions are just not important to him anymore—God is! The rejoicing is "in the Lord" and "in God my Savior."

> *What Habakkuk was unable to do,*
> *the Lord enabled him to do.*

Is it any wonder then that Paul can declare with the same inspired insight: "Rejoice in the Lord always. I will say it again: Rejoice!" (Philippians 4:4), and "I can do everything through Him who gives me strength?" (Philippians 4:13).

It is obvious to even the casual reader of these three chapters that Habakkuk is a changed individual. The emotional outbursts of frustration and anger are no longer present. He is no longer pointing his accusing finger at God for delaying intervention and/or lacking concern, but he is now raising his arms in praise to God. He is not complaining, but celebrating!

> *He is not complaining, but celebrating.*

I do not know what Habakkuk heard or saw while waiting for the Lord to answer his concerns. I believe that God came to him. How God comes doesn't matter. It matters that He comes. The prophet attempted to describe God's visitation in Hebrew poetry, but language is too inadequate to share such mystical experiences. However, the outcome of the divine visitation is obvious. Habakkuk, in a clear and concise affirmation of faith, states the source and the substance of his newfound strength.

How God comes doesn't matter.
It matters that He comes.

"The Sovereign Lord" is the source of the prophet's strength. "This is the only place outside the Psalms (16:2, 68:20, 109:21, 140:7, 141:8) that the phrase *yahweh 'adonay* ("Sovereign Lord") occurs, expressing the divine personal name preceded by His title. The names emphasize the power and majesty of God. Habakkuk uses the strongest names for God available" (Baily and Barker, p. 376). Habakkuk is precise: His strength is a gift from the Lord. The strength to cope with the challenges and to "rejoice in the Lord" is divinely imparted. The prophet makes it known that his response to the difficulties of life, no matter how severe, is not of his own doing.

The substance of his strength is indicated with familiar illustrations. He states that the Lord "makes my feet like the feet of a deer, he enables me to go on the heights." Habakkuk uses the image of the female deer known for its surefootedness in uneven and mountainous terrain. This deer can walk and jump among the crags and cliffs with full confidence in its skill and agility. It is able to escape danger because of its swiftness and balance in the uneven places. "To go on the heights" refers to the high places—perhaps a reference to the mountainous areas high above most danger and predators.

God's gift of strength enables Habakkuk to remain sure footed in his very insecure world. It helps him to keep his balance when he walks the narrow, perilous precipices of life. God makes it possible for him to scale the mountain peaks like a skilled and experienced climber. Because the Lord is his strength, Habakkuk can celebrate his victory over all the dangers and all the enemies he may face in life.

God's imparted strength takes him to new spiritual heights where he can sing his victor's song.

The Mystery of His Song

Habakkuk's inspiration for this song is not self-generated. He doesn't decide that from now on this will be his response to the vicissitudes of life; he cannot, nor can we, create melodious music of passionate praise to God by our individual effort.

I recall my question to our Marine group commander during an arduous fifteen-mile hike with full packs in the North Carolina summer heat and humidity. "Colonel, why are we doing this? We will never walk fifteen miles in a combat situation."

I will never forget his response: "Chaplain, this training builds character, develops resolve, and makes Marines. We want Marines to learn that when their body tells them they cannot take another step, they do it anyhow. This teaches them to endure." I learned what he meant: going on, one step in front of the other, notwithstanding the heat, humidity, blisters, aching muscles, and the battle of the will. This is "toughing it out."

Habakkuk, however, is not talking about "toughing it out" through positive thinking, positive imaging, and mind over matter. Although that is an important skill we all need to develop, Habakkuk is referring to music of the soul. He is describing "singing in the rain." God has given to him a song for all seasons. His heart is bursting with joy.

Habakkuk is not prescribing a response to suffering expected of everyone. He does not deliver a prophetic word to people in precarious predicaments to maintain an attitude of joy through it all. It is not his intention to mandate a rule or a principle. Habakkuk is celebrating because his spiritual life was renewed through a divine visitation, and with a fresh outlook on life, he can only rejoice.

We can, however, learn from this prophet's experience. God can give to anyone a spiritual song for all situations of life. His coming to us might not be the dramatic visitation the prophet had. Whether in a church or a "watchtower" of our own choosing, God will come to those who diligently seek Him and patiently wait for Him. He can endow the human heart with joy and embrace the human spirit with hope. If we, like Habakkuk, take our burdens to the Lord in humble and sincere prayer, honestly seek spiritual renewal, and expectantly wait for God's coming, we will be satisfied with the salvation of the Lord. Mysterious music will fill our souls, and we also will rejoice in the Sovereign Lord.

Abba, Father

How lonely are some days and nights!
Life's journey here is fraught
With hardships, trials, temptations, too—
Tough questions, troubling doubt.
As young ones run to loving arms
When tears for hurt are shed,
We must cry, "Abba, Father,"
Like lambs for whom He bled.
Our Lord who loves us more than life
Will comfort, save, and heal;
As we lean heav'ly on His breast
—Surrender to His will.
And we His children evermore
Shall know we are His own,
Through valleys of the shadow—
On to His great white throne,
Where we shall gather and rejoice
In victory over death—
Where hurt and sin are vanquished,
By His eternal breath.
Milliner, D. (p. 22)

CONCLUSION

There are no indicators to determine how much time transpired from the anguish of Habakkuk's intense interrogation of God to the joy of his spiritual renewal. There may be days, months, or even years between chapter 1 and chapter 3 of the book. There is no prescribed time for a sufferer to move beyond questioning to a quest for God's intervention. Every person is different and each personal response to crisis is new and different. There are those minor events which require little change to our normal coping response. However, there are also those major ordeals that demand all of our mental resolve and all of our inner resources and more.

It cannot be expected that someone could face the calamity of the proportion Habakkuk speaks and immediately begin praising God. Neither should anyone encourage or instruct a sufferer to praise God anyhow. God has gifted humans with an array of emotions. We are not to deny our feelings, but to own them as gifts of God. Our anger and grief as well as other emotions need to find appropriate expression. However, we learn from Habakkuk that we can choose to seek God, to silence our soul before Him and to experience His presence and strength. God then can help us move beyond our frustration, fear, and fury, to joy and jubilation. God can gift us with the spirit of rejoicing.

God is there all the time. His presence is always with us. However, I have assisted those who were so critically challenged by their personal crises that their emotions shut down and they felt nothing. When there was even a small sign of anger or sadness, it was cause for joy. They were beginning to feel again. Others, ventilate their feelings immediately. However, for many, it might take weeks, months, and even years before they can open up their soul to God. This release cannot be forced. Emotional blocks have to fall one by one. Questions of God and anger toward God need to be addressed and may need to be expressed before healing can occur and hope is restored.

Drs. Michael and Kathy Langston chronicle their journey from the invisible wounds of war to spiritual healing in their excellent book, *A Journey to Hope: Healing the Traumatized Spirit*. Chaplain Langston was a colleague who served after me in Camp Fallujah, Iraq (2007–2008). I wept reading the book that details his emotional, mental, and spiritual struggle with PTSD. I understood clearly. Kathy offers the perspective of the warrior's spouse. The wound of Mike's soul was deep; the family struggles were significant, but the journey to hope and healing was celebrated. Like me, Mike continues to deal with his PTSD, but his refreshed and renewed faith in God has taught him to sing a new song from a deeper place of surrender and hope.

Habakkuk shows us the possibilities. He could have remained in the chapter—one phase of his life indefinitely. I know those who have remained mad at God; their lives became stagnant; they could not move on and would not seek needed assistance to get out of their downward-spiraling freefall. The spiritual trauma destabilized their lives, and finding meaning in their misery was missing. Some are more able to endure severe suffering by will power alone and continue to function effectively; however, they are still in "chapter 1" living.

Habakkuk moves to the chapter-two phase. He has expressed his deepest feelings and stated plainly his complaints to God. He intentionally decides to give God an opportunity to address him and his concerns. He purposely determines to set his heart and soul to the reception mode. He is willing to listen to God; he knows he can't keep living in chapter 1. Over time the questions and anger would have devastating effects on his life. He sincerely wants to move forward, so he waits for God. He receives the word "the just shall live by faith." God has made known to him that he must continue to be faithful to God even without answers to his questions. Habakkuk is in the chapter 2 phase—stay the course, remain loyal to the faith of his fathers, "tough it out."

Eventually, the prophet desires more. Merely holding on has weakened him. Though he knows the righteous will win in the end, the struggle to survive suffering is taking its toll on him. He begins the chapter 3 phase of his journey. He prays that God would renew, bring to new life, His work. His quest turns from seeking to understand and from trying to endure, to experiencing His God. He opens his mind to spiritual reflection, his heart to spiritual renewal, and his soul to spiritual rejoicing. God visits him in some mysterious manner, giving him strength for the dark and difficult days and assisting him to proclaim, that though the worst of scenarios occur in the land and in his personal life, he will rejoice in the Lord. He attains a new perspective and gained a new power.

> *He opens his mind to spiritual reflection,*
> *his heart to spiritual renewal,*
> *and his soul to spiritual rejoicing.*

God assists all those who take steps in His direction. Though they take hesitant baby steps, the unseen hand of God is present to undergird and guide seekers to Himself. When the steps become more stable, God is still present in the process. He is leading us to the place of ultimate freedom and triumph. Paul said, "I have learned the secret of being content in any and every situation..." (Philippians 4:12b). He suffered terribly. He encountered many tragedies and trials. He prayed three times that God would deliver him from his "thorn of the flesh" (most likely an eye disease). Yet God did not. God said to Paul that His grace was sufficient and His strength would be made complete in weakness. The thorn that tormented Paul and severely impacted the quality of his life was not removed. But though the thorn remained, roses bloomed. Paul learned that the all-sufficient grace of God gifted him with powerful strength and passionate praise.

Grant observes that "trauma is an invitation onto the spiritual path... Healing requires an expansion of meaning" (p. 38). Thus, the "task of every victim is to discover healing and direction in events that not only injure but which have the power to destroy. How to develop hope and spiritual deepening in the midst of despair is a challenge that every survivor must meet" (p. 3).

Paul states that trials of faith can indeed lead to positive and productive growth.

> Therefore we do not lose heart. Though outwardly we are wasting away, yet inwardly we are being renewed day by day. For our light and momentary troubles are achieving for an eternal glory that far outweighs them all. So we fix our eyes not on what is seen, but on what is unseen. For what is seen is temporary, but what is unseen is eternal. (2 Corinthians 4:16–18)

James also writes about the growth through troubles: "Consider it pure joy, my brothers, whenever you face trials of many kinds, because you know that the testing of your faith develops perseverance. Perseverance must finish its work so that you may be mature and complete, not lacking anything" (James 1:2–4). "The emotional power of trauma can be a catalyst for deep processing that can yield beneficial new perspectives" (Calhoun and Tedeschi, p. 69).

The term often used today is posttraumatic growth. Calhoun and Tedeschi explain:

> The frightening and confusing aftermath of trauma, where fundamental assumptions are severely challenged, can be futile ground for unexpected outcomes that can be observed in survivors: posttraumatic growth. The term post-traumatic growth refers to positive psychological

change experienced as a result of the struggle with highly challenging life circumstance. (p. 1)

But the concept is not new to Christians. New Testament writers frequently speak to the growth through suffering. Paul says in Romans, "Not only so, but we also rejoice in our sufferings, cause we know that suffering produces perseverance; perseverance, character; and character, hope" (Romans 5:3, 4). This is post-traumatic growth in endurance, character, and hope.

Peter states that suffering will bring about restoration, strength, firmness, and steadfastness (1 Peter 5:10). William Barclay, in his *The Letters of James and Peter*, observes that the Greek work used here for restore is *kartarizein*, which is most commonly used for restoring a fracture. So Peter is saying that suffering can indeed repair the fractures in our lives and restore health and wholeness. The word used for firmness, *sterixein*, means to make us as solid as granite. "It is a toughness of fibre, a new staying-power, a new power which no demand on him can overcome. He emerges like the toughened steel that has been tempered in the fire" (p. 324). Suffering will strengthen a person. The verb is *sthenoun*, which means *to fill with strength*. Finally, Peter states that through suffering, God will settle a person or make steadfast. The verb is *themelioun*, which means *to lay the foundations*. "It is in life's trials that we discover the great truths on which life is founded, and which we cannot do without" (p. 325).

There is now empirical evidence to support this early Christian view of growth through suffering. Psychologist Jonathan Haidt suggests that "people need adversity, setbacks, and perhaps even trauma to reach the highest level of strength, fulfillment, and personal development" (p. 136). He writes:

> *I don't want to celebrate suffering, prescribe it for everyone, or minimize the moral imperative to reduce it where we can. I don't want to ignore the pain that ripples out from each diagnosis of cancer, spreading fear along lines of kinship and friendship.*

I want only to make a point that suffering is not always bad for all people. There is usually some good mixed in with the bad, and those who find it have found something precious: a key to moral and spiritual development." (p. 141)

Calhoun and Tedeschi are quick to note that pain or distress may never be deemed desirable. They only speak of the growth that has transpired out of the journey (p. 7). They describe posttraumatic growth as

> the experience of individuals whose development, at least in some areas, has surpassed what was present before the struggle when crises occurred. The individual has not only survived, but has experienced changes that are viewed as important, and that go beyond what was the previous status quo. Posttraumatic growth is not simply a return to baseline—it is an experience of improvement that for some persons is deeply profound. (p. 4)

Therefore, the real question that God can help us to ask "is not, why did this happen to me? What did I do to deserve this? This is really an unanswerable, pointless question. A better question would be, 'Now that this has happened to me, what am I going to do about it'" (Kushner p. 136).

Mad at God with sighing is a difficult place for Christians. Who wants to be mad at God? But life happens. A frightful word from our doctor, the pains in our body, the confusion in our minds—so many bad things can and do happen to all of us and we really don't understand the reason. We cannot fathom why God doesn't heal our body or mind, or change our situation. "Why would a loving Almighty Father want His child to suffer like this?" we ask. Sometimes we are paralyzed by our perplexity and ashamed of our fierce anger at God. "How can we be Christian and have these feelings?" we wonder.

Faith in God with singing can come to us. Even in the midst of the storm, we can sing. We can grow. God can empower and enable us to be renewed in our faith, in our minds and in our souls. Like the apostle Paul, we can learn that in all things God can work to transform them for our benefit. God's sufficient grace can lift us to new and improved levels of living when the circumstances don't matter so much—when only our faith in God's goodness and perfect will is paramount. We sing from our soul that our God reigns, and though we may never understand the whys, we can still embrace our faith and learn to rejoice always.

God gives a song to those who wait on Him.

Recovering from post-traumatic spiritual disorder has been an ongoing process for me. Cynicism can be a dangerous road for a Christian to travel. Faith comes and goes as combat memories surface. The traumatized spirit needs time for healing, and the need for divine visitations is constant. Heschel, a Jew exiled from Poland, came to United States in 1940 to teach at Hebrew Union College. He indicated that his aim was to shock modern man out of his complacency and to awaken him to the spiritual dimension which was fading from contemporary consciousness. He wrote that human beings need to recapture a personal awareness of God and of other people by feeling the presence of God "within and beyond things and ideas" (Flescher, p. 298).

So how can modern people regain a personal awareness of God? He observed that a universally accessible feeling is the experience of the sublime—for example, in the presence of the grandeur of nature. A sense of the sublime entails wonder. The person confronts the "ineffable," that which cannot ever be expressed in words. Heschel insists that the ineffable is not a psychological state but an encounter with a mystery "within and beyond things and ideas" (Flescher, p. 298).

Pargament observes that spirituality is "interwoven into the fabric of the everyday. We can find the spiritual in a piece of music, the smile of a passing stranger, the color of the sky at dusk, or a daily prayer of gratitude upon awakening" (p. 3). Indeed, these can be visits of God.

Sometimes, His presence is in a song on Christian radio, a word from Scripture, a sermon, or a meditative devotional. I often feel His nearness on long bicycle rides outside where nature renews me. He can be present in a rabbit eating grass alongside the road, a doe and her "Bambi" crossing into the woods, horses surveying their pasture, or cows gathering near a favorite watering spot. I feel Him in the warmth of sun on my face, and I hear Him in the quiet voice of the breeze. The smell of freshly cut hay and sight of tall corn stalks reaching up to the sky declare His handiwork all around me. While watching the birds at my feeder or two doves sitting on a fence, I am reminded that His eye is on the sparrow an not one falls without His knowing. A majestic sunrise or a calming sunset proclaims the glory of our Creator God. The turning colors of autumn, the silent snow on a winter's eve, the bright azaleas of spring, and my blooming caladiums in midsummer—all witness changing seasons designed by an unchanging God. Just sitting on my deck and listening to the cacophony of night sounds draws me nearer to the One who made me.

Sometimes God looks over my shoulder when I watch my wife playing tea party with our granddaughter or listen to grandsons telling about their sporting events. I can be blessed by a Facebook post, a text from colleague or friend, or an inspirational book. I can just hold and pet my dogs and feel God's love for me reflected in my love for them. I can be cycling on the beautiful California coast or in the mountains of West Virginia and feel closer to heaven. Participating in an organized biking event with my cycling partner and good friend brings a joy, God-given.

Sometimes God comes in an undeniable and powerful way as He came in a vision to Isaiah and in His likeness to Moses. In those times His presence is like a "mighty, rushing wind." But often, He comes in a "still, small voice." He speaks to us whenever and wherever we seek Him. His mini visits are enough to warm my soul and to remind me of my Creator, His greatness and power. They are still sublime encounters of our mighty God.

The following two poems from *NightSongs* describe how God's majestic creation can inspire and uplift our spirits.

Silence of the Snow

Monday's usual frantic pace,
Back to work and harried race—
To do and do while checking lists,
Making sure that nothing's missed....
The silent snow, a sweet surprise,
Has slowed the pace and halted drives
As we are granted a reprieve
From hectic schedule. What relief
To lie in bed and extra hour,
To muse on bird and snow-flaked bower
While lacey whites do cast their spell,
A lovely hush on field and dale,
A gentle blanket's call to rest.
"Be still" is heaven's soft request—
"Be still and know that I am He
Who shaped the world, created thee.
Give pause to racing heart and mind;
Listen, and in calmness find
An anchorhold, a moment's peace,
In which you find a sweet release
Of stress, of fear, anxiety—
Breathe deep', know joy, claim
hope, be free!" (*NightSongs*)

In the Mountains

Sitting on the porch in early morning,
I saw wisps of translucent cloud
as night's dew rose in
mists of amethyst.
Within a vast aviary, a myriad
of bird songs lifted
praise heavenward
while a woodpecker's steady percussion kept the
symphony earthbound.
The fragrance of mountain laurel invited the
hummingbird's ballet,
And as he quenched his desire for nectar,
I drank deeply of Nature's elixir.
Sensing God's presence in my
morning sanctuary, I
worshipped Him
and rose renewed in spirit for the
days ahead.(*NightSongs*)

In Fallujah, Iraq, my deputy and I would stop on the way to the chow hall and observe ducks in the pond. Simply, ducks. Swimming and prancing. But the scene gave us a sense of sanity and humanity in a dangerous and uncertain environment. Marines befriended dogs in all the villages to connect with their feelings and to some sense of normalcy. These were visits with God.

Songwriters Rodney Clawson, Monty Criswell, and Wade Kirby penned George Strait's 2015 No. 1 country hit, "I Saw God Today." Criswell had mentioned that after unsuccessful hunting trips, he would state to others that he "caught a glimpse of God today" even if he had nothing to show for his time or efforts. In the song, the writers note that God's "fingerprints are everywhere" and if we only take time to slow, to look, to consider, we may be able to proclaim, "I Saw God Today."

Yes, God can certainly surprise us with mini divine visits at any time if we are just open to looking and expecting. When I fully appreciate that God is indeed everywhere, then I can be open to seeing and hearing from Him in all places and times. These visits renew faith and revive a crushed spirit. A song can form in the heart and then on the lips. I can celebrate peace, *shalom*, and "mount up on eagles' wings and I can declare that my help comes from the Lord. O, the nagging, perplexing questions may remain." The post-traumatic stress disorder does not disappear. But like Paul, I have learned to honor and embrace my questions. It is spiritual freedom to no longer need answers, but to wholly trust God. Jesus prayed desperately in the Garden of Gethsemane, "If it is possible, take this cup of suffering from me" *but* "not my will but yours be done."

We like Habakkuk, can rise to faith
and move from sighing to singing.

Habakkuk moved from *sighing to singing*. He moved from complaining to God to celebrating in God. Habakkuk moved from being mad at God to a sustaining faith in the Lord God. God had come to the prophet. His coming changed everything. The prophet was enabled to see the suffering differently. He was strengthened to be "more than conqueror." He was given the gift of faith where he could walk the perilous cliffs with balance and confidence and do it with a song. The "thorn in the flesh" has not been removed. The situation of distress may not change. The crisis may be prolonged. The disease may still attack the physical body. Grief may linger. Our questions may not be answered to our satisfaction. But meeting God changes us. It transforms our outlook. We, like Habakkuk, can rise to faith and move from sighing to singing. Yes, whatever transpires, we can sing because God is present with His power and might.

Sacred Silhouettes

We shun the shadows of the day
That hinder, cloud, darken our way—
Not trusting pain, problem or ill,
We wonder how it is God's will
That we should suffer and endure
Those things that injure and obscure
Our sense of peace and joy and light
And make us tremble in the night.
Then as we cry to God in fear,
Seek comfort and allow the tears
To cleanse our doubt as sure' we must
The Holy Spirit breathes on us,
Reminding all to cast our cares
Upon the One who surely bears
Us and them on eagle's wings
And gives our hearts a song that sings.
When fright, perplexity, and shame
Are lifted up in His great name;
Like object held before the light,
The shade becomes a silhouette.
Obscurity then takes a form,
Unknowing then becomes informed,
And we can smile at revelation
When God unveils the tribulation
As creative action, shaping force
That surely will then chart our course.
(Milliner, *Pearl Haven: By the Sea*)

Now to him who is able to do immeasurably more than all we ask or imagine, according to his power that is at work within us, to him be glory in the church and in Christ Jesus throughout all generations, for ever and ever! Amen. (Ephesians 3:20–21 NIV)

Praise

Great Father of the Universe,
Lord of Heaven and Earth;
How wondrous are Thy mercies,
Matchless is Thy Truth—
I Magnify Thee!
Thou Deliverer of Daniel,
Provider of my needs,
Kind Shepherd of the Psalmist,
My hungry soul doeth feed—
I Praise Thee!
O Jesus, Lamb of Calvary,
Resurrection's Morning Star,
Lily of my valley,
Lord, Savior, and Master—
I Love Thee!
Sweet Spirit, Dove, O Holy Ghost,
Power of Peter and Paul,
Strength unto my weakness,
Comfort to my soul—
I Bless Thee!
Hallowed God, my Maker, Thou
Creator of the Day,
Giver of Life, of Love, of Peace,
My joy-filled heart must say—
I Thank Thee!

Donna Milliner
Used by Permission

PHOTO APPENDIX

On Our Way into the Theater of War

Ready to Go Visit my Chaplain Teams

Guns Firing

Prayer before Convoy

In a Tent at Forward Operating Base

Drawing Strength and Comfort from God's Word

Visiting Sites

Camp Fallujah Chaplain Leadership Team

Sandstorm

Duck Pond in Camp Fallujah

Humanitarian Project

Direct mortar hit on chapel space.

Memorial of Sgt. John M. Smith

One of many Memorial Services We Conducted

My Cycling Partner Margaret Grun Kibben

My Wife and Partner in Ministry Donna Milliner

My Boys

Named after me, Chaps, is my true therapy dog.

REFERENCES

Baily, W., & Barker, K. (1998). *The New American Commentary: Micah, Nahum, Habakkuk, Zephaniah.* B & H Publishing Group.

Barclay, W. (1958) *The Letters of James and Peter.* Philadelphia: The Westminster Press.

Bergin, A. E. (1983). Religiosity and mental health: A critical reevaluation and meta-analysis. *Professional Psychology*, 14, 170–184.

Calkins, R. (1947). *The Modern Message of the Minor Prophets.* New York: Harper and Brothers.

Calhoun, G., & Tedeschi, R. G. (2013) *Posttraumatic growth in clinical practice.* New York: Routledge.

Flescher, A. M. (2003). *Heroes, Saints, and Ordinary Morality.* Washington, DC: Georgetown University Press.

Funk, M. M. (2013). *Thoughts Matter: Discover the Spiritual Journey.* Collegeville, Minnesota: Order of Saint Benedict Press.

Gailey, J., and Kelly, B. *The Layman's Bible Commentary: Micah, Nahum, Habakkuk, Zephaniah, Haggai, Zechariah, Malachi.* United States, John Knox Press.

Gall, T. L., Charbonneau, C., Clarke, N. H., Grant, K., Joseph, A. & Shouldice, C. (2005). Understanding the nature and role of spirituality in relation to coping and health: A conceptual framework. *Canadian Psychology*, 46, 88–104.

Garcia, D., Glover, B., Lewis, C., Millard, B., Timmons, T. *Even If.* Kobalt Music Publishing Ltd.

Grant, R. (1996). *The way of the wound: A spirituality of trauma and transformation.* Self-published.

Haidt, J. (2006). *The happiness hypothesis: finding modern truth in ancient wisdom*. New York: Basic Books.

Herman, J. L. (1997). *Trauma and recovery*. New York: Basic Books.

Hoge, C. (2010). *Once a Warrior Always a Warrior: Navigating the Transition from Combat to Home*. Guilford, CT: Lyons.

Holy Bible. (1986) *New International Version*. Nashville: Holman Bible Publishers.

Langston, M. W. and Langston, K. J. (2016). *A Journey to Hope: Healing the Traumatized Spirit*. Silverton, OR: Lampion Press, LLC.

Martin-Achard, R., *From Death to Life*. Translated by John Penny. Edinburgh and London: Oliver and Boyd.

Martineau, J. (English philosopher, 1850–1900) *Public Quotes*.

Meichenbaum, D. (1994). *Treating adults with PTSD*. Waterloo, ON: Institute Press.

Milliner, D. (2010). *NightSongs*. Richlands, NC: Reimann Books.

Milliner, D. (2011) *Pearl Haven: By the Sea*. Richlands, NC. Reimann Books.

Pargament, K. I. (2007). *Spiritually Integrated Psychotherapy: Understanding and Addressing the Sacred*. United States: Guilford Publications.

Patterson, J. (1948). *The Goodly Fellowship of the Prophets*. New York: Charles Scribner' and Sons.

Rogers, D. F. (2002). *Pastoral Care for Post-Traumatic Stress Disorder: Healing the Shattered Soul*. NY: The Haworth Pastoral Press, Inc.

Taylor, C. L. (1956). The Book of Habakkuk. *The Interpreter's Bible. Volume 6*. Nashville: Abingdon Press.

BIOGRAPHICAL INFORMATION

Dr. Lee Milliner served as a navy chaplain with ecclesiastical endorsement from The Southern Baptist Convention for twenty-seven years. Over seventeen of those years he spent with the Marine Corps. He served at every level with the Marines. He was a battalion chaplain for Seventh Communications Battalion and First Radio Battalion, Kaneohe, Hawaii, and Headquarters Battalion, Marine Corps Air Station Yuma, Arizona. He was group chaplain for the Brigade Service Support Group 1, Kaneohe, Hawaii, and Second Surveillance and Intelligence Group, Camp Lejeune, North Carolina. He served as division chaplain for the 3D Marine Division, Okinawa, Japan. He had two assignments as Marine Expeditionary Force chaplain, III Marine Expeditionary Force, Okinawa, Japan and Second Marine Expeditionary Force, Camp Lejeune, North Carolina. He was force chaplain for the Multi-National Forces in Western Iraq.

He also served as station chaplain, Marine Corps Air Station New River; and senior chaplain, Marine Corps Installations East; and senior chaplain, Marine Corps Base Camp Lejeune.

His navy assignments included chaplain, *USS Vancouver* (LPD-2); senior Protestant chaplain, Naval Submarine Base, Groton, Connecticut, and director.; pastoral care services, Naval Hospital Camp Lejeune, Jacksonville, North Carolina.

He graduated from Lee University, Cleveland, Tennessee with a bachelor of science, and from Southeastern Baptist Theological Seminary with master of divinity and master of theology (Old Testament Studies). He received the doctor of ministry degree from Luther Rice Seminary, Jacksonville, Florida. Additionally, he attended the Chaplain's Advanced Course with classes at Naval War College and Salve Regina University and was awarded a master of human resources management from Salve Regina University.

He retired from the navy in 2008 and he became a director of the Campbell University Extended Campus, Marine Corps Base, Camp Lejeune and MCAS New River. He taught as adjunct faculty for Campbell University, Camp Lejeune, North Carolina, and Coastal Carolina Community College, Jacksonville, North Carolina.

He pastored Rock Spring Baptist Church in Townsville, North Carolina, and served as interim pastor in Memorial Baptist Church and First Baptist Church in Maysville, North Carolina, and Bear Baptist Church, in Hubert, North Carolina.

He has been married to his wife Donna for forty-nine years. They have three children, April Lee Snyder, Jonathan Milliner, and James Milliner, and six grandchildren.

Mad at God unwraps the mystery of the Old Testament prophet's wisdom through Lee Milliner's own experience as a seasoned military chaplain and combat veteran, and we are given an invitation to peer into the soul of the despairing believer that we may find our own way through perplexity and pain. Heartfelt and heartrending, this book taps into the hard-earned wisdom of scripture in a way that is understandable and affirming. We are allowed to wrestle with the angst and anger that come with facing inexpressible pain and untold sorrow. There are no holds barred... This book tackles the one place few are willing to go: into the eye of the storm that is the crisis of faith. But it's here that recovery is received: real and available for all who have the courage to move toward the salvation found in our Redeemer.

—From the "Foreword" by Margaret Kibben,
Chaplain, House of Representatives
Twenty-sixth Chief of Navy Chaplains

ABOUT THE AUTHOR

D r. Lee Milliner served as a navy chaplain with ecclesiastical endorsement from The Southern Baptist Convention for twenty-seven years. Over seventeen of those years he spent with the Marine Corps. He served at every level with the Marines to include one year in Fallujah, Iraq, as force chaplain for the Multi-National Forces in Western Iraq in 2005–2006.

He graduated from Lee University, Cleveland, Tennessee with a bachelor of science, and from Southeastern Baptist Theological Seminary with a master of divinity and master of theology (Old Testament Studies). He received the doctor of ministry degree from Luther Rice Seminary in Jacksonville, Florida. Additionally, he attended the Chaplain's Advanced Course with classes at Naval War College and Salve Regina University and was awarded a master of human resources management from Salve Regina University.

He retired from the navy in 2008 and he became director of the Campbell University Extended Campus, Marine Corps Base, Camp Lejeune and MCAS New River. He taught as adjunct faculty for Campbell University, Camp Lejeune, North Carolina, and Coastal Carolina Community College, Jacksonville, North Carolina.

He pastored Rock Spring Baptist Church in Townsville, North Carolina, and served as interim pastor in Memorial Baptist Church and First Baptist Church in Maysville, North Carolina, and Bear Baptist Church, in Hubert, North Carolina.

He has been married to his wife Donna for forty-nine years. They have three children, April Lee Snyder, Jonathan Milliner, and James Milliner, and six grandchildren.